MW01015342

A PLACE CALLED
HEAVEN

Surprising Truths About
Your Eternal Home

DR. ROBERT
JEFFRESS

LifeWay Press®
Nashville, Tennessee

Published by LifeWay Press® • © 2018 Robert Jeffress • Reprinted March 2020

ISBN 978-1-4627-6652-9 • Item 005796314

Dewey decimal classification: 236.24
Subject headings: HEAVEN \ FUTURE LIFE \ ESCHATOLOGY

To order additional copies of this resource, write LifeWay Church Resources Customer Service; One LifeWay Plaza; Nashville, TN 37234; Fax order to 615.251.5933; call toll-free 800.458.2772; email orderentry@lifeway.com; or order online at www.lifeway.com.

Printed in Canada

Groups Ministry Publishing • LifeWay Resources • One LifeWay Plaza • Nashville, TN 37234

CONTENTS

ABOUT THE AUTHOR

ROBERT JEFFRESS is the senior pastor of the thirteen-thousand-member First Baptist Church in Dallas, Texas, and a Fox News contributor. He's also an adjunct professor at Dallas Theological Seminary.

Dr. Jeffress has made more than two thousand guest appearances on various radio and television programs and regularly appears on major mainstream media outlets such as Fox News Channel's *Fox and Friends, Hannity, Lou Dobbs Tonight, Varney & Co., and Judge Jeanine,* as well as on ABC's *Good Morning America* and HBO's *Real Time with Bill Maher.*

Dr. Jeffress hosts a daily radio program, *Pathway to Victory,* which is heard nationwide on more than 930 stations in major markets such as Dallas-Fort Worth; New York City; Chicago; Los Angeles; Houston; Washington, D.C.; San Francisco; Philadelphia; and Seattle. His weekly television program can be seen in 195 countries and on 11,295 cable and satellite systems throughout the world, including China, and on the Trinity Broadcasting Network and Daystar.

Dr. Jeffress is the author of twenty-four books, including *When Forgiveness Doesn't Make Sense, Countdown to the Apocalypse, Not All Roads Lead to Heaven,* and *A Place Called Heaven: Ten Surprising Truths about Your Eternal Home.*

Dr. Jeffress led the congregation of First Baptist Dallas to complete a $135-million re-creation of its downtown campus. The project is the largest in modern church history and serves as a spiritual oasis that covers six blocks of downtown Dallas.

Dr. Jeffress graduated from Southwestern Baptist Theological Seminary with a DMin, from Dallas Theological Seminary with a ThM, and from Baylor University with a BS. In May 2010 he was awarded a doctor-of-divinity degree from Dallas Baptist University. In June 2011 Dr. Jeffress received the Distinguished Alumnus of the Year award from Southwestern Baptist Theological Seminary.

Dr. Jeffress and his wife, Amy, have two daughters and three grandchildren.

INTRODUCTION

If any of us learned that we were going to move to a foreign country, we would do everything we could to learn about that place so that we would be prepared when moving day arrived. One day all people will leave this life and enter the next. As Christians, we know someday we'll leave our familiar country and be united with God in heaven. And yet many of us know very little about this place called heaven.

Many of us don't give much thought to heaven because our journey seems so far off. Perhaps we believe we still have time to prepare for our trip, but the reality is that none of us know when we'll be called to our final destination. Some of us may be intimidated by passages of Scripture about heaven that seem hard to understand. Others don't give much thought to heaven because it seems to have very little to do with the way we live today.

For whatever reason, people don't think about heaven as much as they should. Heaven is relevant to our lives today. Thinking about heaven will change the way we live on earth. In this study we'll examine the Scriptures to answer six common questions about heaven so that we'll be prepared when the time for our departure arrives.

HOW TO GET THE MOST FROM THIS STUDY

This Bible study book includes six weeks of content for group and personal study.

GROUP SESSIONS

Regardless of what day of the week your group meets, each week of content begins with the group session. Each group session uses the following format to facilitate simple yet meaningful interaction among group members, with God's Word, and with the video teaching of Dr. Jeffress.

START. This section includes questions to get the conversation started and to introduce the video segment.
WATCH. This section includes key points from Dr. Jeffress's video teaching.
DISCUSS. This section includes questions that guide the group to respond to Dr. Jeffress's video teaching and to relevant Bible passages.

PERSONAL STUDY

Each week provides five days of Bible study and learning activities for individual engagement between group sessions. The personal study revisits stories, Scriptures, and themes Dr. Jeffress introduced in the videos so that participants can understand and apply them on a personal level. The days are numbered 1–5 to provide personal reading and activities for each day of the week, leaving two days off to worship with your church family and to meet as a small group. If your group meets on the same day as your worship gathering, use the extra day to reflect on what God is teaching you and to practice putting the biblical principles into action.

SUPPLEMENTAL ARTICLES

At the back of this book you'll find articles that can further develop your understanding of the ideas presented in this study. They provide additional biblical teachings on key words and doctrines related to heaven.

TIPS FOR LEADING
A SMALL GROUP

INCLUDE OTHERS

Your goal is to foster a community in which people are welcome just as they are but encouraged to grow spiritually. Always be aware of opportunities to—
INCLUDE any people who visit the group;
INVITE new people to join your group.

ENCOURAGE DISCUSSION

A good small-group experience has the following characteristics.
EVERYONE PARTICIPATES. Encourage everyone to ask questions, share responses, or read aloud.
NO ONE DOMINATES—NOT EVEN THE LEADER. Be sure your time speaking as a leader takes up less than half of your time together as a group. Politely guide discussion if anyone dominates.
NOBODY IS RUSHED THROUGH QUESTIONS. Silence isn't a bad thing. People often need time to think about their responses to questions they've just heard or to gain courage to share what God is stirring in their hearts.
INPUT IS AFFIRMED AND FOLLOWED UP. Make sure you point out something true or helpful in a response. Don't just move on. Build community with follow-up questions, asking how other people have experienced similar things or how a truth has shaped their understanding of God and the Scripture you're studying. People are less likely to speak up if they fear you're looking for only a certain answer.
GOD AND HIS WORD ARE CENTRAL. Opinions and experiences can be helpful, but God has given us the truth. Trust God's Word to be the authority and God's Spirit to work in people's lives. You can't change anyone, but God can. Continually point people to the Word and to active steps of faith.

KEEP CONNECTING

Think of ways to connect with group members during the week. Participation during the group session is always improved when members spend time connecting with one another outside the group sessions.

WEEK

1

What Difference Does Heaven Make in Our Lives Today?

Start

Welcome to session 1 of A Place Called Heaven. *Use the following questions to begin your time together.*

> Let's start by introducing ourselves to be certain we all know one another. If you don't know someone, share a little about yourself.

> When you think about heaven, what images comes to mind? What shaped your images of heaven?

> How often do you think about heaven?

Every Christian is on a journey to a place called heaven—a one-way trip that will last for eternity. The subjects of death, judgment, heaven, and hell are often daunting to consider. Most people choose to ignore these topics because they believe they have long lives ahead of them. However, Scripture addresses these inevitable realities on a regular basis. This is why we're committing the next six weeks to gain a better understanding of the place Jesus has prepared for us and to bring heaven closer to our hearts, minds, and everyday lives.

> Before we watch Dr. Jeffress's teaching, would someone open with prayer, asking God to lead us and teach us more about heaven?

Watch

Use these statements to follow along as you watch video session 1.

Our departure for heaven is both certain and relatively soon.

The fact that life is very brief here on earth should motivate us to use our time wisely.

Why Should We Focus on Heaven?
1. Focusing on heaven reminds us of the brevity of our earthly life.

2. Focusing on heaven prepares us for the certainty of judgment.

> There is a way that leads to eternal death.

> There's a more narrow road that leads to heaven.

> There are gates that open to both eternal death and eternal life.

3. Focusing on heaven motivates us to live pure lives.

> Judicial righteousness is our right standing before God.

> When God looks at you and me, he sees us as totally, completely forgiven.

> Ethical righteousness is our right acting before God.

4. Focusing on heaven places suffering in perspective.

Although God's promise for heaven is yet still future, it really should impact the way we live every day.

Video sessions available at LifeWay.com/APlaceCalledHeaven

Discuss

Discuss the video with the group, using the questions below.

How could our daily responsibilities cause us to think less about heaven instead of more?

Have you ever experienced a life event that caused you to focus on heaven or to long for a better place than earth? If so, explain.

Read John 14:2-3. Why did Jesus want the disciples to understand that He was preparing a place for them?

C. S. Lewis once said, "Aim at Heaven and you will get earth 'thrown in': aim at earth and you will get neither."[1] How should the reality of heaven shape the way we live?

When are you most likely to consider the brevity and fragility of your life? Why should those realities cause us to think more seriously about heaven?

Read Matthew 7:13-14 and John 14:6. Discuss the similarities between these passages. What do they teach about heaven?

How can we focus on living a pure life without trying to earn our way into heaven?

Why does it seem to be increasingly difficult to live pure lives in our culture? What factors might make a life of purity more challenging today than in previous times?

How does the fact that Christ's righteousness is available to us connect our daily struggle for purity to the reality of heaven?

How does the hope of heaven affect our perspective on suffering (death, tragedy, injustice, etc.)? When has this hope helped you personally?

Read week 1 and complete the activities before the next group session.

1. C. S. Lewis, *Mere Christianity* (New York: HarperOne, 1980), 134.

What Difference Does Heaven Make in Our Lives Today?

Why should we be concerned about heaven? The obvious answer is because we're all going to die and step into eternity.

My ministry necessitates a lot of travel. Every time I journey to a distant destination, I make a checklist of tasks I need to accomplish before I leave and items I need to take with me on the trip. This preparation is especially important if I know I'll be gone for an extended period of time.

For a long international trip, for example, I need to do the following.

- Contact my credit-card company and notify them of where I'll be so that they won't think my card or identity has been stolen and freeze my account.

- Call the cell-phone company to have my phone enabled for international service.

- Check the weather forecast to know what clothing to pack.

- Be certain I have my ticket and passport so that I can arrive at my destination and get past the gates.

Wise travelers go through a routine to prepare for leaving home, even if it's just a weekend getaway. Yet very few people ever prepare for the ultimate journey everyone will take to an eternal destination. Many Christians don't consciously spend a lot of time thinking about heaven. Perhaps you haven't either. The overwhelming responsibilities of living in this world can easily eclipse time spent thinking about the reality of the next life. In addition, the fact that we know so little about our home in heaven makes it seem remote and irrelevant to our earthly lives.

This is exactly why over the next six weeks we'll examine what the Bible tells us about the place Jesus has prepared for those who trust in Him for salvation (see John 14:2-3). My prayer is that through this study you'll not only long for heaven but also live out your days here on earth with a renewed sense of divine intentionality.

DAY 1

THE INEVITABILITY OF DEATH

All people die. The one certainty all people have in life is the fact that it ends. And death often comes suddenly as well as unexpectedly. King Solomon stated:

> *Man does not know his time: like fish caught in a treacherous*
> *net and birds trapped in a snare, so the sons of men are*
> *ensnared at an evil time when it suddenly falls on them.*

ECCLESIASTES 9:12

The Old Testament patriarch Isaac expressed the same dilemma: "Behold now, I am old and I do not know the day of my death" (Gen. 27:2).

If God has ordained every day of your life—including the day of your death—the stark reality is that every second that passes moves you closer to the grave. That's a great reason to begin thinking seriously about your eternal home, as well as how you spend your days on earth.

How often do you consider the inevitability of death? Check one.

❑ Constantly

❑ Rarely

❑ A healthy amount

What emotions or feelings do you have when you think about death? Why could considering death be productive?

What has informed your thoughts on death? Family background? The Bible? Other religious knowledge? Personal loss?

A Place Called Heaven

We've all heard the old saying that became the motto of hedonism: "Eat, drink, and be merry, for tomorrow we die." This has been a common cultural mindset for centuries, and it continues today. However, Scripture warns of continually adopting or following such a perilous paradigm.

Jesus' parables were filled with teaching about seeking God's kingdom, being intentional about life, and investing time and energy in loving people. He taught these truths by both wisdom and warning. Read Jesus' parable of the rich fool:

> *Someone in the crowd said to Him, "Teacher, tell my brother to divide the family inheritance with me." But He said to him, "Man, who appointed Me a judge or arbitrator over you?" Then He said to them, "Beware, and be on your guard against every form of greed; for not even when one has an abundance does his life consist of his possessions." And He told them a parable, saying, "The land of a rich man was very productive. And he began reasoning to himself, saying, 'What shall I do, since I have no place to store my crops?' Then he said, 'This is what I will do: I will tear down my barns and build larger ones, and there I will store all my grain and my goods. And I will say to my soul, "Soul, you have many goods laid up for many years to come; take your ease, eat, drink and be merry." ' But God said to him, 'You fool! This very night your soul is required of you; and now who will own what you have prepared?' So is the man who stores up treasure for himself, and is not rich toward God."*
>
> LUKE 12:13-21

What flawed assumption did the wealthy man make?

How might you be storing up things for yourself that have little or nothing to do with what God desires for you?

Why do greed and materialism distract us from recognizing the inevitability of our death and therefore from preparing for our eternal home?

Jesus wasn't condemning wealth in these verses. The reason He called the man a fool is that he allowed his pursuit of wealth to make him complacent and self-sufficient. In verse 20 the word *required* in the original language of the New Testament comes from the concept of a loan that has come due or has been called in. Our lives are on loan to us, and Jesus can call them in anytime He chooses.

Few of us live with this reality in mind. We must always remember that we aren't promised tomorrow. Often only the threat of terminal illness, a near-miss accident, or a tragedy will make us think about being stewards of the life God has so freely given. But we need to recognize that each breath is also a gift from Him.

Everyone will leave this world at some point. God alone will determine how long we'll be on this earth. The realization that our time is finite should certainly motivate us to use all our time and resources wisely. To avoid being caught off guard like the rich fool, we need to live with the brevity of life and the urgency of eternity in mind:

> *Teach us to number our days,*
> *That we may present to You a heart of wisdom.*
>
> PSALM 90:12

What does it mean "to number our days"? How does numbering our days produce wisdom?

List three areas of life in which you're using the time God has given you as you should.

1.

2.

3.

List three areas of life in which you may be wasting time and could make better use of your precious hours.

1.

2.

3.

Record one practical step you could take to eliminate some items on the second list and maximize the time you devote to items on the first list.

Learning to number our days means we live with the understanding that our time on earth is limited and is expiring with every passing moment. Taking an eternal perspective on our minutes, hours, and days allows us to exercise wisdom in the way we spend our time. Numbering our days helps us live with the end in mind.

Christian author Joni Eareckson Tada, who became a quadriplegic in a diving accident in 1967, wrote:

> Heaven may be as near as next year, or next week; so it makes
> good sense to spend some time here on earth thinking candid
> thoughts about that marvelous future reserved for us.[1]

Joni also encourages believers to invest in relationships. Sharing the truth of the gospel in any way and anywhere we can is always a valuable and eternal use of our time on earth.

What's one simple way you can invest more in your relationships?

What's one simple way you can maximize your time on earth this week by focusing on eternity?

PRAYER

Heavenly Father, I confess that death is a difficult subject for me to think about, so I don't think about heaven enough. Please help me better understand Your purpose for my life and my place in heaven, the eternal home You've promised me. Help me number my days so that I can spend them investing in eternity. In Christ's name, amen.

1. Joni Eareckson Tada, *Heaven: Your Real Home* (Grand Rapids, MI: Zondervan, 1995), 15.

DAY 2

THE BREVITY OF LIFE

One of my closest friends and I both lost our parents when we were young adults. That shared experience has caused us both to talk frequently about the brevity of our time on earth. However, as much as I miss my parents, I see their early departure, from my perspective, as a gift from God that continually reminds me of how brief my own life is. I must live with eternity in mind. And that's true for you as well.

Have you ever lost someone close to you? If so whom?

What impact did that loss have on your understanding of life and death?

If your loved one who died was a Christian, how does his or her death make heaven seem more real to you?

Read James's words about the brevity of life:

> *You do not know what your life will be like tomorrow. You are just a vapor that appears for a little while and then vanishes away.*
>
> JAMES 4:14

Is planning wrong? What point was James making?

Why are we so often consumed with what will happen tomorrow? How has planning for the future caused you to miss opportunities God has given you today?

What makes it difficult for us to accept that our lives are like a vapor?

Planning is wise and is commended in Scripture (see Prov. 14:15; 15:22; 20:18). Jesus sent out disciples with a plan (see Luke 10:1-2). Paul was methodical when establishing churches (see Acts 14:21-23). James wasn't calling believers to stop planning but rather to plan with the brevity of life in mind. We've all had plans that fell through at the last minute. Most people have experienced unexpected hardship. Just like our plans, our lives can change irreversibly without a moment's notice. Like a vapor, life is here for a moment and then is gone.

Read King David's prayer on this topic:

> *LORD, make me to know my end*
> *And what is the extent of my days;*
> *Let me know how transient I am.*
> *Behold, You have made my days as handbreadths,*
> *And my lifetime as nothing in Your sight;*
> *Surely every man at his best is a mere breath.*
>
> PSALM 39:4-5

Why is it good for us to remember how short life is?

In what ways is our perspective on time radically different from God's?

A Place Called Heaven

Consider the following diagram.

Randy Alcorn uses this diagram to illustrate the brevity of life. The line is eternity. The dot represents all your years on earth. Right now you're living in the dot, so to speak. Yet we rarely think about the line, the eternity that's waiting. Millions of lives live only for the dot, which is only a blip on the radar compared to the eternal.[1]

Yet the dot and the line are connected, for our lives touch eternity. While we live in the dot, we don't live for the line. If we aren't careful, we'll begin to see our lives as the dot and not the line. As David said, our days are merely "handbreadths" (v. 5). Against the backdrop of eternity, the dot is minuscule. We must live with eternity in mind and, in particular, with heaven in mind.

What's one practical step you can take this week to create a stronger connection from your dot to eternity?

How could memorizing some of the Scriptures we've examined this week help you keep the brevity of life in mind?

Use the chart to record a few things you've been delaying and ways you can take action on those items in the coming weeks.

What have you been delaying?	How will you take action in the coming weeks?

Barring the unexpected, this week you, everyone in your family, your small group, and everyone living on the earth will be given the same gift from God. Regardless of age, finances, position, nationality, or any other differentiating factors among human beings, we'll all be given 168 hours this week (seven 7 days times 24 hours equals 168 total hours). Time is an equalizer. We can't do anything about the hours that are gone, and we can't do anything about those to come, only the ones we're living in now. Yesterday is in the past, and tomorrow never actually comes, so today is all we have. We need to use God's sacred gift of time—all 168 hours—to focus on eternity with Him through our attitudes and actions as we love Him and love people. Life is short, so we must live it well.

How do you spend the majority of your free time?

Based on what you recorded on the chart, how could you use your free time better or differently?

PRAYER

Dear Father, You alone know the number of my days, so I trust You with my life and my time. Please guide me and teach me to make the most of each gift—every hour You give me breath—to serve You and love all people with whom I come in contact in Your name. In Jesus' name, amen.

1. Randy Alcorn, *Heaven* (Carol Stream, IL: Tyndale, 2004), 436.

DAY 3
THE CERTAINTY OF JUDGMENT

Because of the reality of sin, we're born traveling down the wrong road. We all start this life headed in the opposite direction from God; we hit the ground running from Him. Because of Adam and Eve's initial sin in the garden, we're born into rebellion. The prophet Isaiah put it this way:

> *All of us like sheep have gone astray,*
> *Each of us has turned to his own way.*
>
> ISAIAH 53:6

Sheep are defenseless animals, so a sheep wandering alone is in serious danger. People don't have to do anything to end up in hell when they die. All they need to do is to continue traveling in the same direction they've been traveling since birth.

Read these words of warning from Jesus:

> *Enter through the narrow gate; for the gate is wide and the way is broad that leads to destruction, and there are many who enter through it. For the gate is small and the way is narrow that leads to life, and there are few who find it.*
>
> MATTHEW 7:13-14

Why do you suppose Jesus said the road to destruction is wide and broad, while the road to life is narrow? How have you seen this truth play out in your experience?

In light of Jesus' words, what choice do we all face?

All of us are born on the road of rebellion. All people have found the road to destruction; it's well traveled. To find the narrow gate or the way of Jesus, we must make a decision to make a spiritual U-turn. The Bible calls this reversal *repentance*.

Repentance is a change of mind that leads to a change of direction. Only when people admit that they're on the wrong road can they discover the right road.

Jesus claimed to be the way, the truth, and the life (see John 14:6). Jesus is the only way to find the narrow road. He alone has the keys to the gates to either eternal judgment in hell or eternal salvation in heaven.

The certainty of judgment lies behind each gate. Hebrews 9:27 states, "It is appointed for men to die once and after this comes judgment." There's no escaping the fact that each one of us—Christians and non-Christians alike—will face God's judgment when we arrive at the end of our lives on earth.

The Book of Revelation describes the judgment that awaits those who reject Christ:

> *I saw a great white throne and Him who sat upon it, from whose presence earth and heaven fled away, and no place was found for them. And I saw the dead, the great and the small, standing before the throne, and books were opened; and another book was opened, which is the book of life; and the dead were judged from the things which were written in the books, according to their deeds. And the sea gave up the dead which were in it, and death and Hades gave up the dead which were in them; and they were judged, every one of them according to their deeds. Then death and Hades were thrown into the lake of fire. This is the second death, the lake of fire. And if anyone's name was not found written in the book of life, he was thrown into the lake of fire.*

REVELATION 20:11-15

Why do we need the truth of verses like these even though they may make us uncomfortable?

Why would Satan want people to ignore Bible passages like this?

How can verses like these make you more grateful for the saving grace and mercy of Jesus?

Judgment is more commonly thought of a fate befalling nonbelievers, but Christians aren't exempt from God's judgment. Though all Christians face judgment with the certainty of forgiveness and deliverance, the end of every Christian's life is also a gate, or judgment:

> *We also have as our ambition, whether at home or absent, to be*
> *pleasing to Him. For we must all appear before the judgment seat*
> *of Christ, so that each one may be recompensed for his deeds in*
> *the body, according to what he has done, whether good or bad.*
>
> 2 CORINTHIANS 5:9-10

Why should knowing that all of our actions will be revealed and evaluated in light of Christ motivate us to love and obey God?

What confidence do we have even as we face this judgment?

What differences do you see between these verses and Revelation 20:11-15?

As Christians, we're assured of heaven, but Paul was talking about a day of evaluation and commendation in which Jesus will judge our actions on earth. All we do in our earthly lives has eternal consequences. What an amazing incentive to seek first the kingdom of God and His righteousness (see Matt. 6:33)!

Have you ever been fired from a job for making mistakes or violating the company's protocols? Or on the other hand, have you ever gone through an evaluation and been promoted in a business? The choices we make on the job yield results. When we're assigned the stewardship of a job in a business, putting ourselves first, ignoring the rules, or being apathetic to the boss's goals and desires eventually results in dismissal. Conversely, putting the company first, working hard to meet the organizational goals, and excelling in a job can bring promotion and blessing.

Most people understand what it's like to build a career. This worldly paradigm not only reflects what happens in eternity but also serves as a practical, simple analogy to better understand the verses you've read.

While Scripture passages like these may be difficult to understand, we must always remember that God is "not wishing for any to perish but for all to come to repentance" (2 Pet. 3:9). His desire is to reward all those who live life for His glory in His name. The certainty of judgment shouldn't scare Christians but should push us to honor God with our lives.

Why should the certainty of judgment motivate us to live zealously for God and to share the gospel passionately with the lost?

PRAYER

Father God, use these verses to motivate and inspire me not only to live my life for You daily but also to share my testimony and faith with the people I encounter so that they will come to know You. You don't want me to fear eternity but to have faith in You now and forever. May my life continually reflect the fact that You're my way, my truth, and my life. In Christ's name, amen.

DAY 4

TO LIVE PURE

When I'm asked to do TV interviews for news channels and talk shows, the majority of the time they're filmed in the late afternoon or early evening. Because of the extremely bright lights and high-definition broadcast equipment, I have to concentrate on keeping my clothes clean throughout the day. I tuck a napkin into my shirt collar at lunch to prevent tie stains. I use a wet towel to wipe any dust off my jacket. And just before the camera rolls, someone always runs a lint remover over my clothing. The reason is that any slight imperfections in my attire or appearance will be visible when broadcast in high definition.

The Bible often uses clothing as a metaphor for our spiritual lives (see Isa. 61:10; Mal. 2:16; Jas. 5:2; Rev. 7:14). A day is coming when every Christian's actions will be placed under the perfect eye of God's judgment, and all imperfections in us will be revealed. When that day comes, we want to be prepared. Preparation comes as we live with moral purity:

> *If any man builds on the foundation with gold, silver, precious stones,*
> *wood, hay, straw, each man's work will become evident; for the day will*
> *show it because it is to be revealed with fire, and the fire itself will test*
> *the quality of each man's work. If any man's work which he has built on*
> *it remains, he will receive a reward. If any man's work is burned up,*
> *he will suffer loss; but he himself will be saved, yet so as through fire.*

1 CORINTHIANS 3:12-15

Why did Paul use the analogy of fire as a purifier that reveals the spiritual work we do in our lives?

What truly matters to God at the end of our lives?

As we discussed in day 3, Christians enter judgment with assurance, but they still face judgment. On that day the purity of our hearts and intentions will be revealed. Paul used fire as a metaphor to describe the judgment that will burn away what's impure within us. While straw and dross turn to ashes, metal and precious stones are purified by fire. When the fire burns our impurity away, we're left with only what's pure and acceptable to God.

Every Christian wears two kinds of righteousness that inform the way we live out our purity. The first is our judicial righteousness—our right standing with God—that we receive when we trust Christ as our Savior. Judicial righteousness is the gift of God's forgiveness; therefore, we can do nothing to improve it, soil it, or remove it. It's the foundation of our purity before the Lord.

Judicial righteousness alone presents an incomplete picture of righteousness. Our changed hearts must result in changed actions. Ethical righteousness is the way we live as Christians—right actions before God after we're saved. Ethical righteousness is the outworking of judicial righteousness:

> *Let us rejoice and be glad and give the glory to [God], for the marriage of the Lamb has come and His bride has made herself ready. It was given to her to clothe herself in fine linen, bright and clean; for the fine linen is the righteous acts of the saints.*

> REVELATION 19:7-8

What's the connection between wearing fine linen wedding clothing and our righteous acts done on earth?

Why is the analogy of a bride at a wedding particularly helpful for us in understanding what it means to prepare ourselves for heaven?

The church is the bride of Christ. Like a bride on her wedding day, we want to offer ourselves to our bridegroom as pure and presentable. This means we must take care to live consistent, ethical lives that prepare us to meet our Savior.

No one today would argue that we live in an increasingly sinful world. We're surrounded by messages and images of immorality, rebellion, and lawlessness that make it hard to keep our character clean and to stay away from the saturation and stench of sin. This daily struggle gets more and more difficult as the days go by. Yet one of the best ways to keep our lives spotless is by allowing our longing for heaven to drive us to be clothed with the pure, righteous character of Christ:

> *Now you also, put them all aside: anger, wrath, malice, slander, and abusive speech from your mouth. Do not lie to one another, since you laid aside the old self with its evil practices, and have put on the new self who is being renewed to a true knowledge according to the image of the One who created him. So, as those who have been chosen of God, holy and beloved, put on a heart of compassion, kindness, humility, gentleness and patience; bearing with one another, and forgiving each other, whoever has a complaint against anyone; just as the Lord forgave you, so also should you.*
>
> COLOSSIANS 3:8-10,12-13

List all the ways Paul said we're to live our ethical righteousness. What do we put on? What do we take off?

How does our judicial righteousness (our hearts changed by God) affect our ethical righteousness (our works from faith)?

When Paul used the phrases "put them all aside" (v. 8) and "put on" (vv. 10,12), he was intentionally referring to taking off dirty clothes and putting on clean ones. What do you need to put off now that you've been changed by Christ?

Much of what we spend our time on will be burned up in the judgment. Our acts of faith, however, will endure beyond this world. That's why living a life of moral purity is essential. It matters not only in this life but also in the next. The metaphor of taking off and putting on clothes shows us that moral purity is a choice we make daily:

> *Since all these things are to be destroyed in this way, what sort of people ought you to be in holy conduct and godliness, looking for and hastening the coming of the day of God, because of which the heavens will be destroyed by burning, and the elements will melt with intense heat! But according to His promise we are looking for new heavens and a new earth, in which righteousness dwells. Therefore, beloved, since you look for these things, be diligent to be found by Him in peace, spotless and blameless.*
>
> 2 PETER 3:11-14

Through Christ we've received the privilege and the power to live lives pleasing to Him by choosing Him over sin. Purity is possible to ready us for heaven by the saving grace of our Savior.

When is it easiest for you to live out your ethical righteousness? What barriers exist to your living the life of purity God has called you to?

PRAYER

Dear Lord Jesus, thank You for Your forgiveness and grace. Thank You also for the power You provide me to live a holy life, choosing Your ways over my own. Help me understand that heaven can begin here with my choices to glorify and honor You. Give me the strength and boldness to say no to the world and say yes to You. In Your name, amen.

DAY 5
THE STRUGGLE OF SUFFERING

I've been a pastor for many years, and one of the questions I'm asked most frequently is "Why does God allow _____?" Insert in the blank any number of horrific experiences that can happen in this life. Sometimes these questions arise from spiritual struggles and doubts, while others result from tragic personal experiences. We all have these questions at different points in our lives for various reasons.

Although God rarely answers the *why* of these questions, He gives us plenty of counsel to help us put suffering in perspective:

> *Momentary, light affliction is producing for us an eternal weight of glory far beyond all comparison, while we look not at the things which are seen, but at the things which are not seen; for the things which are seen are temporal, but the things which are not seen are eternal.*
>
> 2 CORINTHIANS 4:17-18

Remember, Paul had been shipwrecked, imprisoned, and beaten within an inch of his life, yet he referred to each event as "momentary, light affliction" (v. 17).

What was Paul communicating about eternity in these verses?

Why is taking an eternal perspective on struggles hard for us?

We certainly have struggles and heartaches in this world that we feel may never end, yet Paul said that compared to eternity, these agonies are only momentary. Our afflictions, no matter how unbearable they may seem at the time, are light when compared to the weight of heaven.

Would you consider a two-thousand-pound block of concrete to be light or heavy? The answer depends on what you compare it to. Compared to you and me, even weighed together, the block is very heavy. But placed against a fully fueled 777 jetliner, that same concrete block is light. Paul is telling us that perspective is everything. The most horrendous experiences we may suffer through in this life last only a moment compared to the indescribable future God is preparing for us in heaven.

Heaven is the promise that God will eventually make all things right and that He will one day fulfill our deepest longings. Although God's promise is still in the future, it should make a tremendous difference in our lives today. The hope of heaven is that all creation will receive what it has long desired: freedom from the crushing oppression of sin:

> *The anxious longing of the creation waits eagerly for the revealing of the sons of God. For the creation was subjected to futility, not willingly, but because of Him who subjected it, in hope that the creation itself also will be set free from its slavery to corruption into the freedom of the glory of the children of God. For we know that the whole creation groans and suffers the pains of childbirth together until now. And not only this, but also we ourselves, having the first fruits of the Spirit, even we ourselves groan within ourselves, waiting eagerly for our adoption as sons, the redemption of our body. For in hope we have been saved, but hope that is seen is not hope; for who hopes for what he already sees? But if we hope for what we do not see, with perseverance we wait eagerly for it.*

ROMANS 8:19-25

What four truths did Paul identify about creation in these verses?

1.

2.

3.

4.

List two benefits Paul said we'll experience.

1.

2.

The world is fallen. All creation is waiting for God to redeem it because it was subjected to futility, but one day God will release it from corruption. Until that point it groans as in the paint of childbirth. Paul was explaining that right now in their present state, before the return of Christ, both humankind and creation are suffering because of the realities of sin and evil. But in Christ we have hope, and "in hope we have been saved" (v. 24).

One of the greatest examples of suffering depicted in the Bible is Job. God told the entire heavenly realm, including Satan, that Job was "a blameless and upright man, fearing God and turning away from evil" (Job 1:8). He was blessed in every manner a man could possibly be blessed. In a discussion between God and His enemy that's difficult for us to understand, Satan was allowed to take everything from Job. Observe Job's response:

> *Job arose and tore his robe and shaved his head,*
> *and he fell to the ground and worshiped. He said,*
> *"Naked I came from my mother's womb,*
> *And naked I shall return there.*
> *The LORD gave and the LORD has taken away.*
> *Blessed be the name of the LORD."*
> *Through all this Job did not sin nor did he blame God.*
>
> JOB 1:20-22

What strikes you about Job's response to losing everything dear to him?

What view of God must Job have had to respond this way?

Eventually, God frankly spoke to Job, whose response is a great lesson for us all:

> *Job answered the LORD and said,*
> *"I know that You can do all things,*
> *And that no purpose of Yours can be thwarted.*
> *'Who is this that hides counsel without knowledge?'*
> *Therefore I have declared that which I did not understand,*
> *Things too wonderful for me, which I did not know.*
> *'Hear, now, and I will speak;*
> *I will ask You, and You instruct me.'*
> *I have heard of You by the hearing of the ear;*
> *But now my eye sees You;*
> *Therefore I retract, and I repent in dust and ashes."*

JOB 42:1-6

How would you summarize Job's experience with God? What observations can you glean from his words?

God rarely gives us the *why* for suffering. We have no indication in Scripture that Job ever knew anything about God and Satan's exchange. Yet Job exhibited incredible faith, honesty, and transparency throughout his grief and disease. God blessed him with twice what he had lost. Job lived another 140 years, seeing the births of four generations (see v. 16).

Job never received the answers he sought, but he remains an example of patient faithfulness. When we struggle in suffering, we need the same perspective that God gave Job. Seeing all our suffering in light of God's larger plan allows us to wait patiently and faithfully in the midst of hardship.

PRAYER

Heavenly Father, while I pray against any form of suffering, I know it will come into my life. Give me the strength and foresight to be prepared in Your Spirit, just as Job was. Help me place suffering in the proper perspective, knowing that in heaven there will be no more tears or pain. Thank You for eternal life. In Christ's name, amen.

WEEK

2

Is Heaven
a Real Place?

Start

Make sure everyone is acquainted if people attend who weren't present last week.

Would anyone like to share insights from our discussion last week?

What did you learn from last week's personal study? Share insights or questions with the group.

The tales of near-death experiences are intriguing to us. The phrase "near death" is used because if people actually die, they can't come back to relate what happened to them. Many books have been published by people who claim to have died, returned, and want to report what they experienced. Documentary TV shows and based-on-a-true-story movies are also consistently released on this topic.

But what does the Bible say about these experiences? What are we to make of these claims from a Christian perspective? Today we'll investigate these so-called near-death experiences.

Before we watch Dr. Jeffress's teaching, would someone open with prayer, asking God to guide us into His truth and into the light of His Word?

Watch

Use these statements to follow along as you watch video session 2.

Why Are We Fascinated with Near-Death Experiences?
1. A natural curiosity about the unknown
2. Our longing for heaven

Every word needs to be tested by the truth of God's Word.

Seven Principles for Evaluating Near-Death Experiences
1. Remember, near death is not death.
2. The Bible is sufficient.
3. Adding or taking away from the Bible is condemned by God.
4. Question the identity of any being of "light."
5. Beware of the occult.
   Any claims of psychic powers or unusual abilities like clairvoyance
   and telepathy are associated with Satan himself.
6. Jesus' death and resurrection are central to any revelation from God.
7. The Bible doesn't record any near-death experiences.

Four Reasons Paul's Encounter Was Not a Near-Death Experience
1. Paul was very much alive.
2. The light Paul saw was real light that blinded him for days.
3. Paul never remotely gave any description that resembled a near-death
   experience.
4. Jesus gave Paul the mission of preaching the exclusive message of salvation
   through Jesus Christ.

Why Has God Restricted Information about Heaven?
1. He knows that heaven is so far beyond our imagination, human words
   can only diminish the glory.
2. If we knew what was awaiting us, we couldn't wait to get out of here.

Video sessions available at LifeWay.com/APlaceCalledHeaven

Discuss

Discuss the video with the group, using the questions below.

Why do you suppose our culture is so fascinated by near-death experiences?

Have you ever read about any of these so-called near-death experiences? What's your acquaintance with them?

Why do you suppose our culture is more likely to believe a great story—regardless of whether or not it's true—than to consider what the Bible teaches?

In 1 John 4:1 why would God encourage us to "test the spirits" to see whether they're indeed from Him? What might this testing look like in practice?

Read Hebrews 9:27. What's the difference between near death and actual death?

Read Revelation 22:18-19. How do near-death experiences violate this command? Why do so many Christians enthusiastically receive these accounts?

Why do you think the truth and power of the gospel—the crucifixion, burial, and resurrection of Christ—always need to stay central in the way we discern and process truth or revelation in our lives?

According to Dr. Jeffress, why wasn't Paul's encounter with Jesus on the Damascus road a near-death experience?

How does the knowledge that no near-death experience is recorded in the Bible affect your thinking on the many near-death stories being presented today?

In light of today's teaching, how will you respond differently to these accounts in the future?

Read week 2 and complete the activities before the next group session.

Is Heaven a Real Place?

The most definitive answer to the question about the reality of heaven is found in John 13–14. In the waning hours of His earthly life, Jesus sat down with His disciples for a final Passover meal. At some point during this gathering, He got up and began to wash the disciples' feet. After He had finished, He told the group that one of them would betray Him.

Jesus was troubled because He knew the cross lay in wait for Him. Now the disciples were also troubled because their hearts were suddenly filled with many questions about their future. But then Jesus offered some of the most hope-filled words found in Scripture:

> *Don't let your hearts be troubled. Trust in God, and trust also in me. There is more than enough room in my Father's home. If this were not so, would I have told you that I am going to prepare a place for you? When everything is ready, I will come and get you, so that you will always be with me where I am.*

> JOHN 14:1-3, NLT

When Jesus told the disciples about His "Father's home" (v. 2, NLT), He used language that described a real location. Jesus also referred to there being "enough room" (NLT), "many rooms" (NIV), or "many dwelling places" (NASB). The Greek word can be translated as *habitat, lodging,* or *domicile,* and it almost always indicates a locatable, inhabited space. In other contexts it refers to a city, a region, or an individual residence.

Jesus also said He would go "to prepare a place for you" (v. 2, NLT), referring to the creation of something tangible. The concrete language He used in this passage has both the definition and connotation of a real, physical place.

Based on this information, doesn't it seem like nonsense to imagine that when Jesus ascended into heaven in front of many witnesses that He went into a metaphysical state of mind? Doesn't His own language indicate that He went from one physical location—the Mount of Olives—to another physical location—heaven?

DAY 1
HEAVEN IS REAL

When Jesus told the disciples that He was going to prepare a place for them, they didn't understand what He was communicating. Thomas was open about his confusion, asking, "No, we don't know, Lord. ... We have no idea where you are going, so how can we know the way?" (John 14:5, NLT). In other words, if we don't know the destination, how can we possibly know the direction?

John 14:6 is a very well-known verse, often quoted alone outside the passage. In it Jesus boldly identified His identity as well as His offer to humankind: "I am the way, and the truth, and the life; no one comes to the Father but through Me." If Jesus is the way to heaven and if He is God in human form, when we encounter Christ, we're standing at the doorway to eternity with God.

When did you first come to know Christ as the way?

When you initially believed, how much of your decision to follow Christ was influenced by wanting to go to heaven?

As you've grown and matured in Christ, has your faith become more focused on God's will and mission for you here on earth rather than on enjoying a home in heaven someday? Explain.

At first many of us decide to follow Jesus because we want to go to heaven and live with Him when we die. However, as our faith matures, we begin to see that faith is much more than fire insurance. Faith isn't just about what happens to us when we die but the way we live for God in the here and now. Yet making the here and now the entire focus of our faith is also shortsighted. Anticipation of heaven should shape our faith as well. That's why Jesus said, "I go to prepare a place for you" (v. 2).

You may have a room in your home for guests to stay in when they visit you. At some point when you furnished your house, you had to prepare a place for a guest to stay. When you invite someone to visit, you likely spend time in that room preparing the place for the person to stay, attending to details like fresh bedding, towels, and toiletries.

How does the analogy of preparing your home to receive a guest help you better comprehend Jesus' statement about preparing a place for you?

Why do we often tend to treat biblical teachings on heaven like mystical, foreign ideas when they're actually simple and practical?

How should knowing that Jesus is preparing a place for you shape the way you live now?

We use our smartphones to quickly find locations—real places where we need to go. One reason we think of heaven less frequently than we should is that it doesn't seem like a real place to us. But how real does heaven seem in the following account?

After [Jesus] had said these things, He was lifted up while they were looking on, and a cloud received Him out of their sight. And as they were gazing intently into the sky while He was going, behold, two men in white clothing stood beside them. They also said, "Men of Galilee, why do you stand looking into the sky? This Jesus, who has been taken up from you into heaven, will come in just the same way as you have watched Him go into heaven."

ACTS 1:9-11

What directional words are used in this passage? What does the use of these words communicate about the reality of heaven?

How do these words refute the idea that heaven is only a metaphysical state of mind?

Heaven is a real, physical, historical place where Jesus went. The words in Acts 1:9-11 aren't metaphorical but literal.

The Bible speaks of a present heaven and a new or future heaven. In fact, the Bible uses the word *heaven* in three distinct ways.

1. The first heaven is simply the space above the earth where clouds form and birds fly.
2. The second heaven is what we commonly refer to as outer space, where the other planets and the stars reside.
3. The third heaven represents the presence of God, which Paul referred to when he said, "... to be absent from the body and to be at home with the Lord" (2 Cor. 5:8). This is the place Jesus had in mind when He promised the thief on the cross that he would be in paradise (see Luke 23:43). Paul called this place the third heaven that he was allowed to visit:

> *Boasting is necessary, though it is not profitable; but I will go on to visions and revelations of the Lord. I know a man in Christ who fourteen years ago—whether in the body I do not know, or out of the body I do not know, God knows—such a man was caught up to the third heaven. And I know how such a man—whether in the body or apart from the body I do not know, God knows—was caught up into Paradise and heard inexpressible words, which a man is not permitted to speak.*

2 CORINTHIANS 12:1-4

Paul himself was the man described in these verses. How does knowing that Paul went to heaven give you confidence about the reality of heaven? How did Paul describe what he saw?

A Place Called Heaven

In Paul's day talking about different conceptions of heaven was popular among Greek philosophers. In a city like Corinth, these ideas would have been everywhere. In contrast, Paul asserted that heaven was a real place, not a philosophical idea. He knew because God had shown it to him. This hope of paradise allowed Paul to continue to hope and speak truth despite hardship and opposition. His future home changed the way he lived in the present (see vv. 7-9).

Many retirees buy a plot of land near a lake or in the mountains with the plans of spending their final years there. While they're living in their current home, they're building a new home for their final place of residence. Just as the hope of their future home guides the way they live in the present, our hope of heaven shapes the way we live our lives on earth.

Record your thoughts to complete the following statements.

1. I better understand that heaven is an actual place today because:

2. I believe that Jesus is preparing a place especially for me because:

3. Heaven or paradise feels more real to me now because:

PRAYER

Lord Jesus, thank You for preparing a place for me as I would prepare a guest room for a friend. I'm grateful that You'll allow me to stay there with You for all eternity. Please help me let go of any fears or doubts about my future home with You in paradise. Help me trust what the Scriptures promise about my future home with You. In Your name, amen.

DAY 2

A NEW HEAVEN
AND A NEW EARTH

In day 1 we discussed three ways the Bible describes heaven. Today we'll examine one more. The future or fourth heaven is the one God is preparing right now. This includes the new heaven, the new earth, and the new Jerusalem described in Scripture. This will literally be heaven on earth, the phrase we often use to describe an incredible experience. At the end of time, following the second coming and all the end-time events the Bible describes, the saints who've died from the beginning of time, as well as all who were alive on earth and were taken up in the second coming, will reside together forever with God and all the heavenly beings:

> *I saw a new heaven and a new earth; for the first heaven and the first earth passed away, and there is no longer any sea. And I saw the holy city, new Jerusalem, coming down out of heaven from God, made ready as a bride adorned for her husband. And I heard a loud voice from the throne, saying, "Behold, the tabernacle of God is among men, and He will dwell among them, and they shall be His people, and God Himself will be among them, and He will wipe away every tear from their eyes; and there will no longer be any death; there will no longer be any mourning, or crying, or pain; the first things have passed away." And He who sits on the throne said, "Behold, I am making all things new."*

REVELATION 21:1-5

What will happen to the current heaven and earth? Why should this future event concern us in the present?

A Place Called Heaven

Write down four things God won't allow in the new heaven.

1.

2.

3.

God will replace the current heaven and earth with His new heaven and earth. No longer will there be death, mourning, crying, or pain. He will wipe out the old order and make all things new (see vv. 4-5). The new heaven will be a place that's free from the presence and effects of sin. Followers of Jesus should long for such a place.

Consider what else the Bible teaches about the new heaven and and the new earth.

1. The new earth will be physical. The risen Jesus shows us that resurrected bodies there will be physical. Jesus walked through a locked door, yet the disciples were able to see and speak with Him (see John 20:26). He was in a heavenly state while also still in a recognizable physical form.

2. The new earth will be familiar. Going to the new heaven won't be like moving from your hometown to a foreign country. Just as Jesus was recognizable, the earth will be also. Just as there's a new Jerusalem, other places will also continue to exist.[1]

3. The new earth will allow unbroken fellowship. Because God will have wiped away all tears, death, mourning, and pain, we'll eternally live in His fellowship and in perfect community and union with one another.

Of these three truths, which are you most looking forward to experiencing?

Which truth is most surprising to you? Why?

In the new heaven and the new earth we'll have a new home, the new Jerusalem. This place was described by the prophet Ezekiel in chapters 40–48 and by John in Revelation 21–22. From John's vision we can learn three truths about our eternal home.

1. The new Jerusalem will be eternal. Heaven will not only be home but will also feel like home. And there will no longer be a need to move or be transferred because it will be a forever home (see Rev. 22:5).
2. The new Jerusalem will be Eden restored. The capital city of God is a place not only of peace and protection but also of unimaginable beauty. This is the garden of Eden restored and redeemed (see Rev. 22:2-3).
3. The new Jerusalem will be majestic. In the center of the city will be the throne of God, from which the river of life pours as "clear as crystal" (Rev. 22:1).

Based on what you've learned in this brief study, how does your understanding of heaven need to change?

What's the biggest difference between your previous thinking and what you've learned?

The new Jerusalem differs from the old Jerusalem in a significant way:

> *I saw no temple in it, for the Lord God*
> *the Almighty and the Lamb are its temple.*
>
> REVELATION 21:22

The entire focus of the earthly city of Jerusalem was the worship of God at the temple. This is why the old Jerusalem was at the center of Jewish life. However, the new heavenly city needs no temple because we'll live forever in the presence of God. The entire city will be a temple of the Lord. No longer will there be day or night (see v. 23). The Lamb of God will be the eternal light in this city. Understanding where we're headed helps us faithfully live in the present by encouraging us to fix our gaze on the glory that awaits us.

A Place Called Heaven

What are the changes you're most looking forward to in the new heaven and in the future capital city, the new Jerusalem?

How can the new truths you've learned about heaven affect your daily life?

The reality of heaven that the Bible describes is glorious. The words used are poetic and illustrative because some realities are too great to be expressed by the limitations of human language. Even though the Bible is God's authoritative record of all the information He desires for us to have about heaven, speculation still abounds. People are fascinated by reports of near-death experiences, which we'll examine in the remaining studies this week.

PRAYER

Lord Jesus, reading about the new home You've gone to prepare for me is almost overwhelming. Thank You for loving me enough to provide a future home for me. Thank You that Your presence will be the new temple there. Help me live as a heavenly citizen now, laboring to see Your will come on earth as it is in heaven. In Jesus' name, amen.

1. Randy Alcorn, *Heaven for Kids* (Carol Stream, IL: Tyndale, 2006), 51–57.

DAY 3
NEAR-DEATH EXPERIENCES

Dwight L. Moody, a legendary nineteenth-century American evangelist, had dedicated his life to preaching and teaching the gospel. He had traveled the world sharing the good news of Christ's death and resurrection in revivals where thousands heard him preach. But on December 22, 1899, Moody died in his Northfield, Massachusetts, home.

What makes Moody's death interesting is that he may have gained a glimpse of heaven before his actual death. According to the story published in *The New York Times*, Moody said, "I see earth receding; Heaven is opening; God is calling me."[1]

Based on reports by those who've had near-death experiences (NDEs) and by those who study them, Moody's description of seeing earth fading, as if he were outside his body and traveling through space, and heaven looming before him, is a classic near-death experience.

Raymond Moody, the father of the NDE craze and the great-nephew of the famous evangelist, believes his uncle had a near-death experience, a term he coined in his 1975 best seller, *Life after Life*. His seminars on near-death experiences and the popularity of his book fostered a movement that today includes the International Association for Near-Death Studies (IANDS), a research foundation that began in 1981. IANDS defines NDEs as "a profound psychological event that may occur to a person close to death or, if not near death, in a situation of physical or emotional crisis. Because it includes transcendental and mystical elements, an NDE is a powerful event of consciousness."[2]

There's one important difference between the near-death experiences Raymond Moody described and the experience his uncle had. D. L. Moody never came back after his death to tell people what he had seen in heaven.

Why do you think some people are fixated on near-death experiences?

Have you ever studied them yourself? If so, what did you hope to gain?

Let's take a look at one of the most well-known biblical accounts involving death to get Jesus' perception of it:

> *A certain man was sick, Lazarus of Bethany, the village of Mary and her sister Martha. It was the Mary who anointed the Lord with ointment, and wiped His feet with her hair, whose brother Lazarus was sick. So the sisters sent word to Him, saying, "Lord, behold, he whom You love is sick." But when Jesus heard this, He said, "This sickness is not to end in death, but for the glory of God, so that the Son of God may be glorified by it."*
>
> JOHN 11:1-4

If you're unfamiliar with this account, Lazarus in fact died, and Jesus raised him. For what purpose did Jesus use the death of Lazarus?

Why is it important to understand that Jesus uses death for His glory?

> *This He said, and after that He said to them, "Our friend Lazarus has fallen asleep; but I go, so that I may awaken him out of sleep." The disciples then said to Him, "Lord, if he has fallen asleep, he will recover." Now Jesus had spoken of his death, but they thought that He was speaking of literal sleep. So Jesus then said to them plainly, "Lazarus is dead."*
>
> JOHN 11:11-14

Jesus said Lazarus was only asleep. What does this language reveal about Jesus' perspective on death?

Jesus is fully sovereign over death. He knows all events that will transpire before a single one occurs. All of life, including death, is meant to glorify God. Because Jesus knew the end before the beginning, He spoke about Lazarus's death in a way that demonstrated both His perspective on it and His perfect control of the outcome:

Jesus, again being deeply moved within, came to the tomb. Now it was a cave, and a stone was lying against it. Jesus said, "Remove the stone." Martha, the sister of the deceased, said to Him, "Lord, by this time there will be a stench, for he has been dead four days." Jesus said to her, "Did I not say to you that if you believe, you will see the glory of God?" So they removed the stone. Then Jesus raised His eyes, and said, "Father, I thank You that You have heard Me. I knew that You always hear Me; but because of the people standing around I said it, so that they may believe that You sent Me." When He had said these things, He cried out with a loud voice, "Lazarus, come forth." The man who had died came forth, bound hand and foot with wrappings, and his face was wrapped around with a cloth. Jesus said to them, "Unbind him, and let him go."

JOHN 11:38-44

What did Jesus want to teach everyone gathered at Lazarus's grave?

Why is this not a near-death experience but an actual death and resurrection?

The point of this account isn't to explain a near-death experience but to give glory to the one who's sovereign over death. Lazarus was dead; the language used doesn't allow for another interpretation. He had been in a tomb for four days. When Jesus called him, Lazarus came out wrapped in cloth, still bound. This isn't the response of a man who was simply asleep but of one who was dead with no expectation of rising. Christ alone is in charge of our life and death. However, some people, considering this fact insufficient, have indulged in all manner of speculation.

Alex Malarkey, the author of one near-death tale, later recanted the story. After writing a best-selling book titled *The Boy Who Came Back from Heaven* about his NDE, he wrote this statement five years later:

> When I made the claims that I did, I had never read the Bible. People have profited from lies, and continue to. They should read the Bible, which is enough. The Bible is the only source of truth. Anything written by man cannot be infallible. It is only through repentance of your sins and a belief in Jesus as the Son of God, who died for your sins (even though he committed none of his own) ... that you can be forgiven [and can] learn of Heaven. ... I want the whole world to know that the Bible is sufficient.[3]

A Place Called Heaven

How could it be easy for people to be drawn to sensational spiritual stories in their search for God or in their faith walk?

In what ways are you tempted to believe the Bible is insufficient?

Here are three questions Christians must ask when evaluating NDEs.
1. Does an NDE contradict the truth of Scripture?
2. Does an NDE glorify God or a person?
3. Does an NDE motivate people to seek the truth of Scripture or just more NDE experiences?

Why is it critical for a Christian to filter not just NDEs but all spiritual matters through the truth of Scripture?

PRAYER

Heavenly Father, guide me, help me, lead me to constantly filter all of life through Your Word. Lead me into Your truth and away from the lies of the world. Thank You that ultimately You control all of life, death, and eternity. Because I rely on You, I want to walk in Your ways. In Jesus' name, amen.

1. "Dwight L. Moody Is Dead," *The New York Times*, December 22, 1899, http://query.nytimes.com/mem/archive-free/pdf?res=9B04E1DA153CE433A25750C2A9649D94689ED7CF.
2. "Key Facts about Near-Death Experiences," International Association for Near-Death Studies, August 29, 2017, https://iands.org/ndes/about-ndes/key-nde-facts21.html.
3. Alex Malarkey, as quoted in Dustin Germain, " 'The Boy Who Came Back from Heaven' Recants Story, Rebukes Christian Retailers," *Pulpit & Pen*, January 13, 2015, http://pulpitandpen.org/2015/01/13/the-boy-who-came-back-from-heaven-recants-story-rebukes-christian-retailers/.

DAY 4
THE BIBLE & NEAR-DEATH EXPERIENCES, PART 1

Many books and movies about near-death experiences, even those produced by Christian publishers and film companies, create the impression that the Bible hasn't given us enough information about heaven. This, of course, isn't the case. In days 4 and 5 we'll explore seven principles that will help us examine the validity of NDEs in the light of Scripture. We'll find that in its teachings on heaven, as in all things, the Word of God is sufficient.

1. NEAR DEATH ISN'T DEATH. We must remember near anything isn't the same as the actual experience. If you're near New York, you have yet to arrive in New York. If you say you're nearing the mall, you aren't saying you're in the mall yet. Therefore, near death isn't fully dead. Cemeteries are filled with people who are all fully dead. As the author of Hebrews wrote, "It is appointed for men to die once" (9:27).

Why do you suppose we assume that near death is experienced by people who've died, gone to heaven (or hell), and returned—in other words, fully died and returned to life?

Why did God make it clear in His Word that humankind is destined to die only once (see Heb. 9:27)?

2. THE BIBLE IS SUFFICIENT. Part of the attraction to books and movies about NDEs is that it gives us specific information that we don't feel the Bible gives us. But this is exactly why we must be so careful with any source that claims spiritual truth, especially when we're seeking to form Christian beliefs. The Bible speaks clearly about the hope of heaven:

A Place Called Heaven

We do not want you to be uninformed, brethren, about those who are asleep, so that you will not grieve as do the rest who have no hope. For if we believe that Jesus died and rose again, even so God will bring with Him those who have fallen asleep in Jesus. For this we say to you by the word of the Lord, that we who are alive and remain until the coming of the Lord, will not precede those who have fallen asleep. For the Lord Himself will descend from heaven with a shout, with the voice of the archangel and with the trumpet of God, and the dead in Christ will rise first. Then we who are alive and remain will be caught up together with them in the clouds to meet the Lord in the air, and so we shall always be with the Lord. Therefore comfort one another with these words.

1 THESSALONIANS 4:13-18

How does the Bible teach us to have hope against the threat of death?

Why is the hope of the Bible more certain and dependable than any so-called near-death experience?

With what words are we meant to encourage one another? Whom could you encourage as they wrestle with the reality of death or with uncertainty about heaven?

Like us, the Thessalonians had lots of questions about the afterlife and the time that preceded the second coming. Paul wrote to answer their questions and to comfort them. Among the reasons people hold on to near-death tales is that they want to know for certain that their loved ones are in heaven. The problem with this thinking is that we don't need NDEs to explain to us what the Bible has already explained sufficiently. The inspired explanation of Scripture is more than enough to encourage us in the hope of heaven. All who've placed their trust in Christ can find their hope in heaven.

3. ADDING TO OR TAKING AWAY FROM THE BIBLE IS CONDEMNED. This statement makes sense only if we believe the Bible is indeed eternal, inspired by God's Spirit, and infallible. But regardless of whether we believe that, the truth is that obeying God's Word brings blessing, and disobeying brings curses. We see this warning spelled out at the beginning and end of the Book of Revelation:

> *Blessed is he who reads and those who hear the words of the prophecy,*
> *and heed the things which are written in it; for the time is near.*
>
> REVELATION 1:3

> *I testify to everyone who hears the words of the prophecy of this book:*
> *if anyone adds to them, God will add to him the plagues which are*
> *written in this book; and if anyone takes away from the words of*
> *the book of this prophecy, God will take away his part from the tree*
> *of life and from the holy city, which are written in this book.*
>
> REVELATION 22:18-19

These verses mean we must question and filter anyone's claims about heaven, hell, God, Jesus, or other eternal matters through what God says in His Word. If someone makes a claim that can't be supported by Scripture, we mustn't believe and accept it. If someone makes a claim that refutes or questions Scripture, we must reject that claim. Scripture is quite clear in what it teaches.

Circle the action words in Revelation 1:3 that teach us how to interact with God's Word.

Why is it critical for believers to be intentional about reading, hearing, and heeding God's Word?

Why do you suppose God would condemn people who would add to or delete His words? What happens when we add to God's counsel?

As a loving Father, why would God want to protect us from lies, untruths, and distortions of His truth?

God's Word is inerrant; it never affirms anything contrary to fact. The Bible is also sufficient, containing all the knowledge God intends for us to have. We don't need another experience or story to verify the claims of Scripture. The Bible alone tells us what we need to know. Stories of NDEs may not claim to supplement Scripture, but that's what they attempt to do. The purpose of these accounts is to give us hope for heaven that has always been available to us in the Bible. We can't take away or add to the truth of Scripture.

Tomorrow we'll continue our study of biblical principles that equip us to evaluate the claims of near-death experiences.

PRAYER

Father, thank You for Your truth and for the life and freedom it brings to me. Give me a hunger for Your Word and teach me how to evaluate the world's claims through what You teach me. You're indeed sufficient for me, and Your Word is sufficient for all knowledge and wisdom I need in my life. Thank You. In Jesus' name, amen.

DAY 5
THE BIBLE & NEAR-DEATH EXPERIENCES, PART 2

Yesterday we discussed three principles for evaluating near-death experiences in the light of Scripture. Today we'll examine four more.

4. QUESTION THE IDENTITY OF ANY BEING OF "LIGHT." Many people who claim an NDE also claim to have encountered Jesus as part of their experiences. Some have even reported that He said things that are contradictory to Scripture. Yet "Jesus Christ is the same yesterday and today and forever" (Heb. 13:8), so we should never expect an NDE to add any information that contradicts Scripture. If these people thought they met Jesus, but the spiritual being was lying, then who was it?

The Bible speaks of antichrists—counterfeit Christs or imposters—and Jesus warned us about them. The apostle Paul also warned:

> *Even Satan disguises himself as an angel of light.*
>
> 2 CORINTHIANS 11:14

Christian author Isamu Yamamoto speaks to this very subject:

> Spiritual warfare … is a battleground where it is often difficult to identify the enemy. Frequently he disguises himself as a beloved friend. Deception has always been this way, and it has been a deadly weapon in his arsenal evident since he used it in the Garden of Eden. Indeed, Paul warned Timothy that "in later times some will abandon the faith and follow deceiving spirits and things taught by demons" (1 Tim. 4:1 [NIV]). Of course, the most evil deception is when the Devil appears to be God.[1]

The concept of a terrorist's blending into society until it's time to attack has become a common strategy in every nation. But this isn't a new tactic. God's enemy doesn't care what he has to do or how long he has to wait to pull off his plan as long as he can keep someone from turning to God and going to heaven. If an NDE story can keep people from truly knowing Christ, he will use that event for his purposes as well.

Have you ever had an encounter you thought was good only to see in hindsight that it wasn't so good? If so, what was the turning point that led you to see the truth?

Why would Satan and his demons want to disguise themselves as light rather than reveal who they truly are?

How can you use Scripture and this teaching point to avoid being spiritually deceived?

When Paul was in Corinth, false teachers came and promoted a false gospel that claimed to have all the benefits of the gospel but without any of the suffering (see 2 Cor. 11:4). Though these teachings had features in common with Paul's teaching, they were ultimately false, and Paul identified the devil as their author. People with dangerous teachings don't identify themselves; they masquerade as teachers of light. We need to test every spirit to determine whether it's from God (see 1 John 4:1).

5. BEWARE OF THE OCCULT. Many NDE testimonies have far more in common with occult practices than anything we find in the Bible. The occult is a group of religious practices that rely on mystical or magical beliefs. They emphasize the supernatural or a deep interest in the paranormal.

Why are people in our culture fascinated by the occult as a form of entertainment?

If an NDE or another spiritual experience hasn't followed the truth of Scripture or has even refuted the Bible, there's a strong chance that the demonic realm is at play, disguised as light. Many out-of-body experiences that occult members describe sound exactly like NDEs. After having NDEs, many people claim to have developed clairvoyance (the ability to see something about the past, present, or future beyond natural means) and telepathy (the ability to send or receive thoughts from or to another person).

Read Luke's account of an encounter the apostle Paul had with a demonic spirit:

> *It happened that as we were going to the place of prayer, a slave-girl having a spirit of divination met us, who was bringing her masters much profit by fortune-telling. Following after Paul and us, she kept crying out, saying, "These men are bond-servants of the Most High God, who are proclaiming to you the way of salvation." She continued doing this for many days. But Paul was greatly annoyed, and turned and said to the spirit, "I command you in the name of Jesus Christ to come out of her!" And it came out at that very moment.*

ACTS 16:16-18

What types of activities does the account of Paul and the slave girl remind you of today?

What might be some reasons the evil spirit decided to call attention to Paul and Silas?

When we hear about voices beyond the grave, it's possible something supernatural is happening, but the source of that activity isn't God but the devil. The slave girl had a spirit of divination, but it wasn't given to her by God. Scripture universally condemns such practices among God's people (see Deut. 18:10; 1 Sam. 28:8; 2 Kings 17:17; Mic. 3:11). We shouldn't be so eager for information beyond the grave that we consult demonic sources.

6. JESUS' DEATH AND RESURRECTION ARE CENTRAL TO ANY REVELATION FROM GOD.
While NDEs purport to give the people who experience them transcendent or
mystical knowledge of what happens beyond the grave, all true revelation of God
features Jesus at its center. Some people have described the events of Acts 9 as an
NDE, but this conclusion is wrong for several reasons, which are outlined below.

> As [Saul] was traveling, it happened that he was approaching
> Damascus, and suddenly a light from heaven flashed around him;
> and he fell to the ground and heard a voice saying to him, "Saul,
> Saul, why are you persecuting Me?" And he said, "Who are You,
> Lord?" And He said, "I am Jesus whom you are persecuting, but
> get up and enter the city, and it will be told you what you must do."
>
> ACTS 9:3-6

If you've ever heard of or read any accounts of NDEs, what seemed
to be the focus of these accounts?

Why might some people call Paul's conversion an NDE?

What reason do we have to believe that this wasn't an NDE?

Four important points illustrate that Paul's circumstance wasn't an NDE.
1. Paul never claimed to have died. He stayed very much alive throughout
   the entire experience.
2. The light was physical, not just metaphysical, because Paul was literally blinded
   for days.
3. When recalling his experience to others, Paul never mentioned anything that
   sounds like a typical NDE.
4. Through this encounter Jesus commissioned Paul to spread the gospel and end
   his efforts to purge it. Forbidden or mystical knowledge was never the focus.

Why must the gospel of Christ be a filter through which we sift any life
experience?

7. THE BIBLE DOESN'T RECORD NEAR-DEATH EXPERIENCES. Here's a list of people who
died and were brought back to life in the Old and New Testaments. It's clear from
the accounts that these people actually died and didn't have NDEs. In none of these

situations did the person come back and report what he or she saw or experienced "on the other side."

- Elijah and the widow of Zarephath's son (see 1 Kings 17:17-24)
- Elisha and the Shunammite woman's son (see 2 Kings 4:18-37)
- Ezekiel and the valley of dry bones (see Ezek. 37:1-14)
- Jesus and Jairus's daughter (see Matt. 9:18-19,23-26; Mark 5:22-24,35-43; Luke 8:41-42,49-56)
- Jesus and the widow of Nain's son (see Luke 7:11-15)
- Peter and Tabitha (see Act 9:36-42)
- Paul and Eutychus (see Acts 20:6-12)
- Unnamed saints (see Heb. 11:35)

All biblical resurrections point to the power of God and seek to bring people to faith in Him. The most amazing resurrection from the dead, of course, was that of Jesus Christ. Afterward when He spent time on earth, He didn't reveal anything about heaven, likely because He had taught so much about it throughout His ministry. Instead, His focus was on the kingdom of God:

> *To these He also presented Himself alive after His suffering,*
> *by many convincing proofs, appearing to them over a period of*
> *forty days and speaking of the things concerning the kingdom of God.*

ACTS 1:3

What was the subject of Jesus' postresurrection communication? Based on Jesus' example, what should your focus be during the days you have left on earth?

PRAYER

Dear Lord Jesus, my prayer today is that You'll help me discern and reject the false teachings of the enemy. Keep my mind and heart completely focused on You and Your kingdom.

1. J. Isamu Mamamoto, "The Near-Death Experience, Part 2: Alternative Explanations," *Christian Research Journal,* summer 1992, http://www.iclnet.org/pub/resources/text/cri/cri-jrnl/web/crj0098a.html.

Do Christians Immediately Go to Heaven When We Die?

Start

Welcome to session 3 of A Place Called Heaven. *Use the following questions to begin your time together.*

What questions came to mind as you worked through last week's personal study?

What's one truth you've learned about heaven?

The fear of death is a universal human characteristic. Even for Christians, simply the fear of the unknown—what happens after your last breath—can bring much anxiety. In addition, a variety of interpretations and opinions exist in evangelical Christian circles about what happens to believers after they die. In today's video teaching Dr. Jeffress wants to offer hope as well as to clear up some of that confusion.

Before we watch Dr. Jeffress's teaching, would someone open with prayer, asking God to bless our time together today?

watch

Use these statements to follow along as you watch video session 3.

There's one fate for everybody. That is death. But there are two different destinies—heaven or hell.

Death is not the end. It is just the beginning of our eternal reunion with God.

I prefer to be once for all absent from the body so that I can be once for all at home with the Lord.

The moment we leave this body, we are forever at home with the Lord.

People in the Old Testament were saved by the death of Jesus on the cross for their sins.

Jesus paid that debt for all of us, and that's why some of His final words on the cross were "It is finished."

Not everyone goes to the same location when they die. There is a place of blessing, and there is a place of judgment.

When we die, we immediately begin experiencing either God's blessing or God's wrath. There's not a waiting time for the future.

Believers go immediately into God's presence, and while we are there, we're awaiting that creation of the new heaven and the new earth that will be our permanent destination.

Hades is the temporary waiting place of the unsaved dead. It is a place of horrible torment that begins the moment an unbeliever dies.

The reason their name is not in the Lamb's book of life is they said, "I don't need God's grace. I don't need the blood of the Lamb. I will stand on my own good works to enter into heaven."

Discuss

Discuss the video with the group, using the questions below.

Why do you suppose so many people and even some religions want to ignore the reality of hell?

When have you minimized the existence and reality of hell?

How can embracing the truth that we immediately enter God's presence eliminate the fear and terror of death?

Read Luke 23:43. What does Jesus' statement to the thief teach us about what immediately happens after we die?

If we know God's presence awaits us for all eternity, why do we still struggle with leaving our temporary home on earth?

How can a greater knowledge of death, eternity, and heaven help us anticipate Christ's second coming?

When Jesus said, "It is finished!" (John 19:30), what had He finished? What does that accomplishment mean for us?

How does our culture view God's judgment and wrath? Explain.

How can grasping that nonbelievers are actually telling God that they don't need His grace and can rely on their own works on judgment day help someone better understand the gospel?

If Jesus' death on the cross was a payment available to all people, why did God also make faith a personal choice?

Read week 3 and complete the activities before the next group session.

Do Christians Immediately Go to Heaven When We Die?

Death is the result of the universal condition of the soul that affects us all: sin. However, death is also the doorway to eternity:

> *Being always of good courage, and knowing that while we are*
> *at home in the body we are absent from the Lord—for we walk*
> *by faith, not by sight—we are of good courage, I say, and prefer*
> *rather to be absent from the body and to be at home with the Lord.*
>
> 2 CORINTHIANS 5:6-8

Paul made it quite clear that we're either "in the body" (v. 6), living our lives on earth, or we're "at home with the Lord" (v. 8), meaning we're gone from earth and residing in heaven in the presence of God. Christians are in one of those two places. Living here in the body requires faith to know we'll one day be "at home with the Lord." But after we die and are "at home with the Lord," we no longer need faith because we'll have sight—the ability to see and experience the Lord. Paul boldly stated that he preferred to be with the Lord.

Paul used strong statements of belief to show that he had no doubts and complete certainty of the life to come. One reason he could be so assured was that he had actually seen Jesus on the road to Damascus. Experiencing the resurrected Jesus as He is in heaven gave Paul a unique perspective and confidence that paradise is indeed the next stop in life for a Christ follower.

The goal of this Bible study is to give you the same confidence in God's promise and provision of heaven that Paul had. We can then echo his words:

> *We know that if the earthly tent which is our house is torn down,*
> *we have a building from God, a house not made with hands,*
> *eternal in the heavens. For indeed in this house we groan,*
> *longing to be clothed with our dwelling from heaven.*
>
> 2 CORINTHIANS 5:1-2

DAY 1
WHY THE LIVING MUST DIE

Statistics tell us that 3 people die every second, 180 every minute, 11,000 every hour. Approximately a quarter million people die every day, all of them going to either heaven or hell.[1] That's a sobering thought.

Although we understand that non-Christians fear death because they don't know what awaits them on the other side of the grave, the prospects of death and dying can be unnerving for believers as well. Author and quadriplegic Joni Eareckson Tada wrote:

> I look at my own degenerating body and wonder how I will approach that final passage. Will it be short and sweet? Or long and agonizing? Will my husband be able to take care of me? Or will my quadriplegia better suit me for a nursing home? It's not so much I'm afraid of death as dying.[2]

Without a doubt, the thought of death can fill us with terror and dread. However, knowing our destination when we depart from this life can dramatically diminish that fear.

How would you rate your fear of dying?

1	2	3	4	5	6	7	8	9	10
Terrified								Totally	at peace

What factors contribute to the fear or peace you feel?

All people have eternal souls. We were designed to live forever, and that fact leads to an inevitable question: Why must the living die if God originally created humankind to be eternal beings? The answer is clearly spelled out in two Scripture verses:

A Place Called Heaven

All have sinned and fall short of the glory of God.

All have sinned. All have fallen short of God's standard. *All* includes everyone who
has ever lived, lives today, and will ever exist. In the original language the word
translated "fall short" comes from the idea of an archer who shoots at a target with a
bull's-eye. No matter how good he is at firing the arrows from his bow, there's no way
he can hit the mark every time. In fact, he will likely miss the mark more often than
he will make dead center on the bull's-eye.

In our lives we do good things and accomplish righteous acts, but those are the
exceptions, not the rule. We miss the mark of reaching God's standard, His glory.
None of us can make it to eternal safety.

Romans 6:23 states:

The wages of sin is death.

ROMANS 6:23

The wages—what we receive—for falling short of God's glory is death. When we
miss, whether by commission of sin—doing the wrong thing—or omission of righteousness—not doing the right thing—the wages for those moments is death.

Romans 6:23 also says:

But the free gift of God is eternal life in Christ Jesus our Lord.

ROMANS 6:23

Falling short and deserving death make the *but* in Romans 6:23 crucial and critical to
us. The free gift of God changes everything about life and death because eternal life
in Christ is now available. The gift isn't like the wages; while the wages was earned,
the gift was freely given. It's a gift of grace.

When did you first realize that you had fallen short and needed grace?

**How could you explain the grace you've received to someone who's afraid
of death?**

66

How did you know in your heart and life that Christ had saved you?

Recall Joni Eareckson Tada's admission: "It's not so much I'm afraid of death as dying."

What aspects of the process of dying are you afraid of?

How should the gospel of grace provide us comfort even in those moments?

When we think of Jesus enduring His crucifixion and burial, it's easy to quickly shift our focus to the resurrection. But remember that Jesus faced the agony of death and was dead for three days. When we fear dying and death, we have to remind ourselves that our Lord showed us the pattern for His promise that death leads to new life:

> *We have been buried with Him through baptism into death, so that as Christ was raised from the dead through the glory of the Father, so we too might walk in newness of life. For if we have become united with Him in the likeness of His death, certainly we shall also be in the likeness of His resurrection.*
>
> ROMANS 6:4-5

Circle the words *death*, *dead*, and *buried* in these verses.

Why should we identify with Christ not only in His life but also in His physical death?

The death of Christ secured the forgiveness of our sins. His death ensured that we're forgiven in this life and the next. We need to identify with Christ in His death as well as in His resurrection because without death to sin, there can be no resurrection. Death is an unfortunate reality in a world tainted by sin, but believers should be encouraged:

A Place Called Heaven

Precious in the sight of the LORD
Is the death of His godly ones.

PSALM 116:15

Since the children share in flesh and blood, He Himself likewise also
partook of the same, that through death He might render powerless
him who had the power of death, that is, the devil, and might free
those who through fear of death were subject to slavery all their lives.

HEBREWS 2:14-15

What has Christ provided through His sacrifice for us?

In what ways are you currently experiencing freedom from death today?

For Christ to be a perfect substitute for our sin, He had to be like us, even sharing our physical death. Through His death and resurrection, He liberated us from slavery to death and the devil. Knowing this truth, we have no reason to fear physical death. Our death will set us free from the sin and corruption of this world forever.

PRAYER

Heavenly Father, thank You that although I'm still appointed to die once, I can know I'll receive the gift of eternal life with You. I praise You because after I pass through death, I'll see Your face and live with You forever. In Christ's name, amen.

1. Randy Alcorn, *Heaven* (Carol Stream, IL: Tyndale, 2004), xix.
2. Joni Eareckson Tada, *Heaven: Your Real Home* (Grand Rapids: Zondervan, 1995), 201.

DAY 2

WHERE DO CHRISTIANS GO WHEN THEY DIE?

Howard Hendricks, a seminary professor and an author, was well known for his original quotations. One was:

> We are not in the land of the living on the way to the dying. Instead, we are in the land of the dying on our way to the land of the living.

For a Christian, death isn't a termination of life but rather a transition to real life. However, for a nonbeliever, death is the transition to total separation from God.

Think about your unbelieving friends and acquaintances. How would they answer the question "What happens after you die"?

On what do they base their belief in the afterlife?

Scripture is clear that every person, at some point in life, will be presented with both evidence and an opportunity to accept or reject Jesus Christ (see Rom 1:18-24). That's exactly why the Bible describes His offer as a gift (see 6:23). You can refuse to accept a gift. You can refuse to open it. The very concept of a gift means it isn't forced on the receiver but is merely offered. But once we leave this life through death, the opportunity to receive the gift is over. At death our eternal choice is forever sealed.

Earlier in this study we learned that there's a present heaven—"the third heaven" described in 2 Corinthians 12:2. A future heaven is also being constructed for us, as described in Revelation 21:2. The present heaven is temporary, while the future heaven is permanent. The Bible teaches that believers who die today immediately go to the third heaven, where Jesus reigns. We pass from life here on earth into His presence.

Perhaps the most dramatic death recorded in Scripture, other than Jesus' crucifixion, is the stoning of Stephen. While being questioned by the Sanhedrin, he delivered a passionate, knowledgeable gospel presentation connecting Christ to the Old Testament patriarchs. Read about the Pharisees' response:

> *When they heard this, they were cut to the quick, and they began gnashing their teeth at him. But being full of the Holy Spirit, [Stephen] gazed intently into heaven and saw the glory of God, and Jesus standing at the right hand of God; and he said, "Behold, I see the heavens opened up and the Son of Man standing at the right hand of God." But they cried out with a loud voice, and covered their ears and rushed at him with one impulse. When they had driven him out of the city, they began stoning him; and the witnesses laid aside their robes at the feet of a young man named Saul. They went on stoning Stephen as he called on the Lord and said, "Lord Jesus, receive my spirit!" Then falling on his knees, he cried out with a loud voice, "Lord, do not hold this sin against them!" Having said this, he fell asleep.*

ACTS 7:54-60

Why did God allow Stephen to see Him and His glory before a single stone was thrown?

What did Stephen believe about what would happen after His death? How did that knowledge enable him to face death with courage?

Luke made intentional parallels between Stephen's death and Jesus' death. Stephen saw his Lord and knew that he was loved and secure. Stephen is described as falling asleep rather than dying. This term is meant to convey that Stephen was at peace because he knew where he was going. He was going to be with Jesus in paradise.

Let's look once again at a key passage on this topic:

> *Being always of good courage, and knowing that while we are*
> *at home in the body we are absent from the Lord—for we walk*
> *by faith, not by sight—we are of good courage, I say, and prefer*
> *rather to be absent from the body and to be at home with the Lord.*

2 CORINTHIANS 5:6-8

In the language of the New Testament, the statements "We are at home in the body" and "We are absent from the Lord" (v. 6) are in the present tense, representing continuous action. In other words, no one can be in two places at once. Being present in one setting means being absent in another. When we're out running errands, we certainly aren't at home. When we're on the earth, we aren't in the direct presence of Christ.

While this argument might seem obvious and logical, Paul was communicating something about a believer's desire. We can be in one setting but long to be in another. When we're traveling on business, we might long to be at home with our family. For now we must be away, but we want to be somewhere else as soon as we can. When we come to understand and comprehend the reality of what awaits us in heaven, we long to be present there though we must remain here for a while.

In contrast, the phrases "to be absent from the body" and "to be at home with the Lord" (v. 8) indicate actions that are completed. When we return home from our business trip, we can say, "I was traveling, but now I'm finally home. The work is done, and I'm now where I want to be." Once we leave earth and our fleshly bodies, our spirits are transported to our heavenly home where Christ resides. For now we're here, awaiting the transition to our heavenly bodies and our eternal home.

Paul placed the phrase "for we walk by faith, not by sight" (v. 7) right in the middle of these contrasting ideas. Why is faith essential for embracing the hope of heaven?

Have you ever spoken with someone who believed your faith in heaven was misplaced? How did you respond?

All who depart from this earth before the Lord returns will be in the presence of Christ. Likewise, they will all be with Christ when He returns. Paul described the immediate change that the dead in Christ and the Christians alive at Jesus' second coming will experience:

> *Behold, I tell you a mystery; we will not all sleep, but we will all be changed, in a moment, in the twinkling of an eye, at the last trumpet; for the trumpet will sound, and the dead will be raised imperishable, and we will be changed.*
>
> 1 CORINTHIANS 15:51-52

All Christians—those who've died and those who are alive at that time—will receive new, incorruptible, and imperishable bodies that will last for eternity. No aging, sagging, decay, sickness, or disease. Forever young.

Why do you think throughout the generations the age-old tales of a fountain of youth and the search for the secret to everlasting life have been passed down, ignoring the Bible's promises of exactly such a state?

Whom can you tell about eternal life this week? When will you tell them?

PRAYER

Father God, I praise You because while I'm in the land of the dying here, I'm on my way to the land of the living. Thank You that hell and its terrors are no longer my concerns because Jesus is my Savior. Thank You that one day I'll forever be changed and receive an incorruptible body, no longer ravaged by sin and the world. In Jesus' name, amen.

DAY 3

WHERE DID THE OLD TESTAMENT SAINTS GO WHEN THEY DIED?

To fully answer this question, we must understand that all people throughout history—before Christ and after Christ—were saved only one way: through Christ. When someone exercised faith in God's revelation, Christ's payment was credited to their account the moment they believed.

This modern-day analogy may help you understand this concept. When you purchase something but you have no cash to pay for it, you can offer a credit card for the purchase. The retailer accepts the card for future payment by the company that issued you the card. You're assured acceptance of the product or service by credit.

This analogy works well until when we consider the payment. Here's the major difference. Christ not only issued the credit and ensured the payment for sin, but when the bill came due, He also paid it.

Read the verse that best explains Old Testament faith:

> *[Abram] believed in the LORD; and He reckoned it to him as righteousness.*
>
> GENESIS 15:6

What did Abram do? How did God respond?

Abram "believed in the LORD." All saving faith is belief in God's ability to deliver from sin. All believers are saved by Christ. Just like today, anyone throughout history who believed in the Lord, whether Jew or Gentile, was saved by Christ. The following Scriptures help us understand this truth:

> *Jesus Christ is the same yesterday and today and forever.*
>
> HEBREWS 13:8

He has appeared once for all at the culmination of the ages
to do away with sin by the sacrifice of himself. Just as people
are destined to die once, and after that to face judgment,
so Christ was sacrificed once to take away the sins of many.

HEBREWS 9:26-28, NIV

How do these two New Testament verses support Genesis 15:6?
What connections can you find?

Jesus is the single source of salvation for all people in all times. Abraham was saved by faith in Jesus. This truth is consistent with Jewish thinking about the afterlife, which we catch a glimpse of in this parable of Jesus:

Now there was a rich man, and he habitually dressed in purple and fine
linen, joyously living in splendor every day. And a poor man named
Lazarus was laid at his gate, covered with sores, and longing to be fed with
the crumbs which were falling from the rich man's table; besides, even the
dogs were coming and licking his sores. Now the poor man died and was
carried away by the angels to Abraham's bosom; and the rich man also died
and was buried. In Hades he lifted up his eyes, being in torment, and saw
Abraham far away and Lazarus in his bosom. And he cried out and said,
"Father Abraham, have mercy on me, and send Lazarus so that he may dip
the tip of his finger in water and cool off my tongue, for I am in agony in
this flame." But Abraham said, "Child, remember that during your life you
received your good things, and likewise Lazarus bad things; but now he is
being comforted here, and you are in agony. And besides all this, between us
and you there is a great chasm fixed, so that those who wish to come over from
here to you will not be able, and that none may cross over from there to us."

LUKE 16:19-26

What are the differences between Abraham's bosom and Hades?

Abraham's bosom was a place of fellowship and blessing. Lazarus had been received into the company of heaven. Hades, however, was a place of everlasting torment. Here are five key truths about heaven and hell that we can glean from this passage.

1. These two men lived very different lives on earth and in eternity.
2. After death both men immediately went to their eternal destinations.
3. One man immediately experienced blessing and peace, while the other went to suffering and agony.
4. The rich man could see into heaven. We don't know whether the poor man could see into hell, although it's clear that Abraham could.
5. A clear, impenetrable division is in place between these two realms.

One assumption we mustn't make from this story is that rich people go to hell and poor people go to heaven. That wasn't Jesus' point. His intention was solely to show that what we possess or accomplish in this life has nothing to do with our salvation and where we'll spend eternity. Those are determined only by the way we decide to respond to Jesus Christ.

Let's look at the deaths of a few Old Testament patriarchs.

ENOCH

All the days of Enoch were three hundred and sixty-five years.
Enoch walked with God; and he was not, for God took him.

GENESIS 5:23-24

By faith Enoch was taken up so that he would not see death; and
he was not found because God took him up; for he obtained the
witness that before his being taken up he was pleasing to God.

HEBREWS 11:5

Enoch walked with God in a sinful generation. It was his faith in God that saved him. Some interpreters speculate that he was so faithful that God chose to save him from the experience of death and to transport him straight into heaven.

Although Enoch's experience isn't normative, what does it teach us about the relationship between faith and eternity?

DAVID

I have set the LORD continually before me;
Because He is at my right hand, I will not be shaken.
Therefore my heart is glad and my glory rejoices;
My flesh also will dwell securely.
For You will not abandon my soul to Sheol;
Nor will You allow Your Holy One to undergo decay.
You will make known to me the path of life;
In Your presence is fullness of joy;
In Your right hand there are pleasures forever.

PSALM 16:8-11

David wrote that because he had trusted God, he didn't have to be concerned about life or death. God hadn't abandoned him on earth, and He wouldn't abandon him to Sheol. God's pleasures are forever in heaven, and fullness of joy is found only in the presence of God. While this passage is often connected to prophecy about Christ, it's also true of David's relationship with God.

Why should our hope of heaven lead us into consistent joy? How is your faith in Jesus shaping your experience of joy?

PRAYER

Father, I pray David's words as my prayer today: I have set You continually before me. Because You are at my right hand, I will not be shaken. Therefore my heart is glad and my glory rejoices. My flesh also will dwell securely. For You will not abandon my soul to Sheol. Nor will You allow Your Holy One to undergo decay. You will make known to me the path of life. In Your presence is fullness of joy. In Your right hand there are pleasures forever. In Christ's name, amen.

DAY 4

WHERE DO UNBELIEVERS GO WHEN THEY DIE?

Based on all the Scriptures we've studied so far, we know that the current or third heaven isn't the ultimate destination for believers. One day a new heaven and a new earth are coming that will be the final home of all who follow Christ.

Just as the new heaven and the new earth are the final destination for all believers, the lake of fire is the final destination for all unbelievers. Just as the third heaven is the temporary place for believers, Hades is the temporary place for unbelievers. Neither of these is simply a waiting room or a purgatory-type holding room. We know this because Scripture is clear that those who go to heaven experience immediate peace and blessing, while those who go to hell experience immediate pain and agony, as we saw in Jesus' story of Lazarus and the rich man. There's a definite separation between believers and nonbelievers. But we must keep in the forefront of our minds that the true distinguishing feature is that heaven is being in the full presence of God, while hell is total separation from the presence of God and His blessing.

> When we speak or think of heaven and hell, why do we tend to focus on the personal experiences of the two places, such as bliss or agony, rather than the much bigger picture of the presence or absence of God?

Peter wrote a sobering history of God's separating rebellion from righteousness:

> *If God did not spare angels when they sinned, but cast them into hell and committed them to pits of darkness, reserved for judgment; and did not spare the ancient world, but preserved Noah, a preacher of righteousness, with seven others, when He brought a flood upon the world of the ungodly; and if He condemned the cities of Sodom and Gomorrah to destruction by reducing them to ashes, having made them an example to those who would live ungodly lives thereafter; and if He rescued righteous Lot, oppressed by the sensual conduct of unprincipled men (for by what he saw and heard that righteous man, while living among them, felt his righteous soul tormented day after day by their lawless deeds), then the Lord knows how to rescue the godly from temptation, and to keep the unrighteous under punishment for the day of judgment.*

2 PETER 2:4-9

Let's look at a few truths Peter provided.

- God separated Satan and his fallen angels from heaven.
- God separated Noah and his family from the rebellious population.
- God separated Lot from Sodom and Gomorrah.
- God separates from His presence the rebellious who die without choosing Him.
- God can separate you from temptation when you choose Him over sin.

Scripture is clear that only God Almighty is capable of holding rebellion at bay while keeping righteousness securely intact, for on the cross Christ won the war against rebellion.

How can fully placing the focus of our lives on God—on the fact that we'll be either with Him or completely separated from Him for all eternity—bring more clarity and purpose to the way we live our lives day by day?

We'll measure life according to either self or the Savior. By our choices today we're also choosing our future. Choosing not to repent of our sin comes with eternal consequences:

> *Do not be deceived, God is not mocked; for whatever a man sows, this he will also reap. For the one who sows to his own flesh will from the flesh reap corruption, but the one who sows to the Spirit will from the Spirit reap eternal life.*

GALATIANS 6:7-8

In what ways are you sowing to your own flesh? Why is this habit dangerous even for believers who are secure in Christ?

In what ways are you sowing to the Spirit? How does this practice display your saving faith?

What's one practical way you could surrender to God's Spirit some of the areas in which you're sowing to the flesh?

Let's close today by returning to the story of Lazarus and the rich man. After Abraham refused to allow Lazarus to bring him water, the man asked if someone could go and warn his family. Again, Abraham refused by saying:

*If they do not listen to Moses and the Prophets, they will
not be persuaded even if someone rises from the dead.*

LUKE 16:31

We live in a day when everyone has the opportunity to hear and know the gospel, which proclaims that after dying for our sin, Jesus rose from the dead and then ascended to the Father. Understanding the stark, sobering reality of where unbelievers go when they die, we can share the good news of the gospel with them before they perish.

Record the name of at least one person you know who needs Christ. Ask God for the opportunity and the courage to share your faith with him or her.

PRAYER

Lord Jesus, I clearly know and understand that You'll one day separate the righteous from the rebellious. Help me be faithful with Your gospel. Please give me the opportunity to share my faith in You with _____ as soon as I can. Help me live out Your message of salvation as boldly as I can. In Your name, amen.

DAY 5

HEAVEN OR HELL: A FOREVER CHOICE

Jesus taught about the final separation of the righteous from the rebellious, those who've trusted and followed Him from those who've rejected Him:

> *When the Son of Man comes in His glory, and all the angels with*
> *Him, then He will sit on His glorious throne. All the nations*
> *will be gathered before Him; and He will separate them from one*
> *another, as the shepherd separates the sheep from the goats;*
> *and He will put the sheep on His right, and the goats on the left.*
>
> MATTHEW 25:31-33

All is a key idea in this passage:
- All the angels
- All the nations
- All people separated into one of two groups: sheep or goats

Read Christ's response to the sheep:

> *Then the King will say to those on His right, "Come, you who are blessed*
> *of My Father, inherit the kingdom prepared for you from the foundation*
> *of the world. For I was hungry, and you gave Me something to eat;*
> *I was thirsty, and you gave Me something to drink; I was a stranger,*
> *and you invited Me in; naked, and you clothed Me; I was sick, and you*
> *visited Me; I was in prison, and you came to Me." Then the righteous*
> *will answer Him, "Lord, when did we see You hungry, and feed You,*
> *or thirsty, and give You something to drink? And when did we see You*
> *a stranger, and invite You in, or naked, and clothe You? When did we*
> *see You sick, or in prison, and come to You?" The King will answer*
> *and say to them, "Truly I say to you, to the extent that you did it to*
> *one of these brothers of Mine, even the least of them, you did it to Me."*
>
> MATTHEW 25:34-40

What did Christ call the sheep?

Where did Christ send the sheep?

Why do you suppose the sheep didn't know they had served Jesus?

Next read Christ's response to the goats:

> *Then He will also say to those on His left, "Depart from Me, accursed ones, into the eternal fire which has been prepared for the devil and his angels; for I was hungry, and you gave Me nothing to eat; I was thirsty, and you gave Me nothing to drink; I was a stranger, and you did not invite Me in; naked, and you did not clothe Me; sick, and in prison, and you did not visit Me." Then they themselves also will answer, "Lord, when did we see You hungry, or thirsty, or a stranger, or naked, or sick, or in prison, and did not take care of You?" Then He will answer them, "Truly I say to you, to the extent that you did not do it to one of the least of these, you did not do it to Me." These will go away into eternal punishment, but the righteous into eternal life.*
>
> MATTHEW 35:41-46

What did Christ call the goats?

Where did Christ send the goats?

Why do you suppose the goats weren't able to recognize their opportunities to serve Jesus?

Notice that the goats—those who didn't minister in Jesus' name—asked Jesus, "When were You in that predicament and we missed it?" while the sheep—those who ministered in Jesus' name—were evidently accustomed to performing those ministries. These were such normal activities for the sheep that they didn't stand out as anything special. The two group's responses couldn't be more different.

Jesus painted a clear picture of the difference between going to heaven and going to hell. His separation of the sheep from the goats—His true followers versus unbelievers—was based on expressing acts of love to someone in need. Because the sheep knew Christ, they expressed His character in their actions.

Jesus wasn't saying that works saved the sheep but rather that works gave evidence to the world that the sheep belonged to Him. Accepting salvation requires nothing other than expressing faith in Him. Jesus alone saves. We then respond to His free gift by submitting to Him in obedience. Christ followers know they're saved by grace—unmerited favor. Through that grace they're able to join the heavenly Father's kingdom work. Our obedience, action, and works are simply a response to Jesus' gracious gift of salvation.

Followers of Christ aren't saviors, but we're ambassadors of the gospel:

> *We are ambassadors for Christ, as though God were making an appeal through us; we beg you on behalf of Christ, be reconciled to God. He made Him who knew no sin to be sin on our behalf, so that we might become the righteousness of God in Him.*
>
> 2 CORINTHIANS 5:20-21

Ambassadors are officials sent to represent the interests of another. We don't have the ability to save ourselves or anyone else, but we carry God's message of reconciliation with us everywhere we go.

Relationships provide the best opportunities to be Christ's ambassador and share your faith, and your story is the most effective means of sharing. Let's take a few minutes to develop an outline of your personal testimony.

In three to five sentences describe what your life was like before Christ.

Briefly describe the way you came to know Christ. Identify the circumstances and relationships involved in your salvation.

Record in a few short sentences what God has done in your life since that day and ways your life has changed.

Finally, record what God is doing in your life now.

The final component of your testimony will always change as you experience more and more of God. Heaven and hell are permanent destinations. During the time we have left on earth, God gives us the privilege to partner with Him in populating His heavenly home with all people who repent and call on His name for salvation.

Of all your nonbelieving friends, who would be most willing to listen to your testimony? When could you share it?

PRAYER

Lord, Thank You for the salvation, grace, and mercy You've provided. Keep reminding me that both heaven and hell are permanent destinations and that You call me to be Your ambassador of reconciliation to a lost and dying world. Thank You for trusting me with the amazing message of salvation. Help me remain faithful until the day of judgment. In Christ's name, amen.

WEEK

4

What Will We Do in Heaven?

Start

Welcome to session 4 of A Place Called Heaven. *Use the following questions to begin your time together.*

We're at the halfway point in the study. Share one fact about heaven or eternity that you didn't previously know.

Is there a particular Scripture or a new truth you'd like to share from last week's personal study?

Let's face it: there are a lot of misconceptions about heaven, hell, and eternal life. The majority of these exist because opinions and myths have been formed without the illumination of biblical truth. What we'll do in heaven is one of the most misunderstood and misinterpreted of all the questions about life beyond this earth. In this session Dr. Jeffress offers specific answers to common misunderstandings about heaven.

Before we watch Dr. Jeffress's teaching, would someone open with prayer, asking God to reveal His truth to us about the home He's preparing for us?

Watch

Use these statements to follow along as you watch video session 4.

Three Myths about God, Heaven, and Eternity
1. God is a cosmic killjoy.
2. Heaven will be monotonous.
3. Heaven will be one long and unending church service.

Worship will be a central activity in heaven, but it won't be our only activity.

Two Primary Activities in Heaven
1. Heaven will be a place of indescribable worship.

   Worship is the continual awareness of, gratitude toward, and submission to God in everything we do.

2. Heaven will be a place of enjoyable work.

Our Work in Heaven
1. Cultivating
2. Creating

God's will for our vocation is the intersection of our passions and our skills.

Who you are now is who you will be in heaven, minus all the flaws.

Three Perks of Heaven
1. Enjoying other believers
2. Learning more about God
3. Experiencing real rest

Heaven will be a time of enjoying perfect fellowship with one another and that perfect relationship with God we've always longed for.

Video sessions available at LifeWay.com/APlaceCalledHeaven

Discuss

Discuss the video with the group, using the questions below.

Why do you suppose people have so many misunderstandings and misconceptions about what happens in heaven?

How do misconceptions about heaven aid Satan's plan to deceive us?

Why is it easy for us to forget that God gave us work as a gift before the fall?

Dr. Jeffress said heaven will be a place of worship and work. Why don't we associate heaven with meaningful work?

Have you ever thought that heaven would be boring? Why is this idea wrong?

How can we mirror the work of heaven—creating and cultivating—here on earth? How are you performing each task now?

If we define *worship* as "a continual awareness of gratitude toward and submission to God in everything we do," how can this understanding affect our day-to-day lives outside church? When we use this definition, what elements of our lives become worship?

How does the broader spiritual definition of *work* compare with our usual, secular viewpoint? What are some similarities and differences?

How exciting is it to think your passions here on earth will shape the meaningful work you do in heaven?

Among the saints you know who are in heaven, with whom are you looking forward to sharing a relationship there?

Read week 4 and complete the activities before the next group session.

What Will We Do in Heaven?

The myths and misconceptions about heaven that have been passed down through generations range from comical to crazy. As with so many other biblical teachings, the ignorance of and apathy about scriptural truths have not only created these lies but have also brought them to a major level of acceptance by the masses. Here are a few widely accepted schools of thought.

- Heaven is boring, while hell is exciting.
- Heaven is one very long church service, while hell is one big party.
- God is a party pooper, while Satan is the life of the party.

Satan has used these untruths to sow confusion and to divert people from the realities of both heaven and hell, with the ultimate goal of keeping them from a relationship with Christ and God's intended home for them in heaven.

In Matthew 25 Jesus concluded a parable about eternal rewards with this verse:

> *His lord said to him, "Well done, good and faithful servant;*
> *you have been faithful over a few things, I will make you ruler*
> *over many things. Enter into the joy of your lord."*
>
> MATTHEW 25:23, NKJV

In this verse we see God's heart for all people throughout every generation:

- To say, "Well done"
- To compliment and bless them with the words "good and faithful"
- To offer them an inheritance of ruling as Adam originally had
- To usher them into eternal joy in His presence

These truths, taken directly from Scripture, beautifully display both the worship and the work we'll experience in heaven. No boredom, only excitement. No monotony, only majesty. No more pain and sorrow from the remnants of hell, only peace and security from the realities of heaven.

DAY 1

THREE POPULAR MYTHS ABOUT GOD & HEAVEN

The idea that heaven is a boring place has long been a popular myth. Science-fiction writer and atheist Isaac Asimov embraced that belief, once remarking:

> I don't believe in the afterlife, so I don't have to spend my whole life fearing hell, or fearing heaven even more. For whatever the tortures of hell, I think the boredom of heaven would be even worse.[1]

This paradigm comes directly from the enemy's deception to keep people from Christ and His home. Today we'll look at the three most popular myths.

MYTH 1: GOD IS A COSMIC KILLJOY

This myth is based more on misconceptions about Satan than about God. Here are the arguments that support this myth.

- Hell is a never-ending party.
- God is a perennial party pooper.
- Satan is the life of the party.
- Heaven is a dull place.
- Hell is an exhilarating experience.

Here are two strong biblical truths that refute this myth.

1. Satan is a created being, with no ability to create or be original. He can only distort, dilute, and destroy the truth.
2. God is the Creator of all things beautiful, enjoyable, and exciting. He creates every sunrise and sunset and all things in between.

What other misconceptions have you heard people express about heaven?

While everyone knows the widely accepted biblical truths about heaven, such as streets paved with gold, no sorrow, and no pain, how do myths like the previous one gain traction in our culture?

Consider the way Jesus characterized Satan:

> *You are of your father the devil, and you want to do the desires of your father. He was a murderer from the beginning, and does not stand in the truth because there is no truth in him. Whenever he speaks a lie, he speaks from his own nature, for he is a liar and the father of lies.*

JOHN 8:44

How does the truth of this verse address the first myth?

Satan is the father of lies. Deception is at the core of his identity. He lives to spread lies about God. Satan is satisfied when people believe heaven is less than God intended it to be. Jesus correctly stated that there's no truth in Satan. His deceptions are to be rejected, not believed.

MYTH 2: HEAVEN WILL BE MONOTONOUS

This myth derives from the old phrase "Too much of a good thing,"[2] originally attributed to William Shakespeare, meaning the excessive experience of anything, even a good thing, can eventually be harmful.

Our entertainment-driven culture only adds to the idea that doing anything over and over again will become monotonous. But this belief actually shows us that the problem is not the majesty and magnificence of heaven but us.

Another popular phrase could be applied here: "Only boring people get bored." Children today, with endless entertainment options available at the press of a button, get bored just as easily as children in previous generations, if not more so. Boredom is strictly and obviously a personal perception.

What are some ways cultural dilemmas such as monotony and boredom adversely affect our spiritual lives?

Why do people quickly forget the reality of eternity in hell when they adopt myths about heaven?

The apostle John's vision of the new heaven and the new earth refutes the idea that heaven will be monotonous:

> *He who sits on the throne said, "Behold, I am making all things new." And He said, "Write, for these words are faithful and true." Then He said to me, "It is done. I am the Alpha and the Omega, the beginning and the end. I will give to the one who thirsts from the spring of the water of life without cost. He who overcomes will inherit these things, and I will be his God and he will be My son."*
>
> REVELATION 21:5-7

In what ways does this passage provide a guarantee against monotony and boredom in God's kingdom?

God is making all things new. Heaven is a place where all things work as they're supposed to. That makes heaven a place of enjoyment. Our thoughts, desires, intentions, and actions will be free from the burden of sin. In addition, God is infinite, so we'll continually learn and experience new things about God. This biblical picture of heaven is far from monotony.

MYTH 3: HEAVEN WILL BE ONE LONG CHURCH SERVICE

This is probably the most widely believed myth, even among Christians. One reason might be that the only spiritual activity many people see is the church's corporate gathering each week. So if we're in the direct presence of God forever, why wouldn't we be engaged in a church service all the time?

While we were certainly created for worship and will engage in praise and celebration in heaven, that's not the only purpose of our lives in heaven. Today as we go about our usual business, we can stop at any time, even on our busiest days, and worship God and pray. We don't have to be in church to take part in worship or prayer, because God's Spirit lives in us as the temple of the Holy Spirit (see 1 Cor. 6:19). In the same way, our lives in heaven will be full and complete, with worship being only one part—albeit an important part—of our days. Take note of Isaiah's experience inside the throne room of God:

A Place Called Heaven

In the year of King Uzziah's death I saw the Lord sitting on a throne, lofty and exalted, with the train of His robe filling the temple. Seraphim stood above Him, each having six wings: with two he covered his face, and with two he covered his feet, and with two he flew. And one called out to another and said,
"Holy, Holy, Holy, is the LORD of hosts,
The whole earth is full of His glory."

ISAIAH 6:1-3

List ways Isaiah's experience is vastly different from your Sunday-morning church service, the mythical perception most people have of heaven.

On the left side of the chart, record what you used to believe about heaven. On the right side, record what you've come to believe as you've participated in this study.

What I Used to Believe	What I Now Believe

PRAYER

Father God, the lies we've adopted about You and Your heaven must be heartbreaking for You because heaven is actually much more amazing than anything we could possibly experience in this fallen world. Help me be ready to explain an accurate perspective on the wonders of heaven to all people I come into contact with. In Christ's name, amen.

1. Isaac Asimov, as quoted in Randy Alcorn, *Heaven* (Carol Stream, IL: Tyndale, 2004), 409.
2. William Shakespeare, *As You Like It*, ed. John W. Cunliffe and George Roy Elliott (New York: Henry Holt, 1911), 4.1.123–24.

DAY 2

TWO PRIMARY RESPONSIBILITIES: WORSHIP & WORK

Adam and Eve were in direct communication and companionship with God every day. This relationship allowed for pure, personal worship of God at all times.

In the garden of Eden, God gave Adam the two primary responsibilities of worship and work. Without sin all of Adam's life was worship, including his work. He reflected God by the work he did. In that sense his work was worship:

> *The LORD God planted a garden toward the east, in Eden; and*
> *there He placed the man whom He had formed. Out of the ground*
> *the LORD God caused to grow every tree that is pleasing to the*
> *sight and good for food. Then the LORD God took the man and*
> *put him into the garden of Eden to cultivate it and keep it.*
>
> GENESIS 2:8-9,15

God gave Adam a clear responsibility. In modern terms he was a produce farmer, specializing in fruits and vegetables. God would cause the plants to grow as Adam cultivated and kept them all. This was a partnership from the beginning until Adam broke the agreement.

In what ways are our lives still similar today to this same arrangement, even in a fallen world?

How did sin's entrance into the world affect worship and work?

When Christ returns and God establishes the new heaven and the new earth, our lives will return to this same original arrangement with our Creator and Redeemer—worshiping and working in the kingdom of God. Seeing Jesus Christ face-to-face in all His glory will totally change our worship:

A Place Called Heaven

I looked, and I heard the voice of many angels around the throne and the living creatures and the elders; and the number of them was myriads of myriads, and thousands of thousands, saying with a loud voice, "Worthy is the Lamb that was slain to receive power and riches and wisdom and might and honor and glory and blessing." And every created thing which is in heaven and on the earth and under the earth and on the sea, and all things in them, I heard saying, "To Him who sits on the throne, and to the Lamb, be blessing and honor and glory and dominion forever and ever." And the four living creatures kept saying, "Amen." And the elders fell down and worshiped.

REVELATION 5:11-14

Circle all the words that describe the number of worshipers in heaven.

Underline all the words that describe Jesus.

Worship in heaven is radically centered on Jesus. How is that both like and unlike our worship on earth? Why is such worship never boring?

Rather than being a rare exception to the rote, programmed activity too many church-goers engage in on most Sundays, the kind of worship John described will happen every time we're in God's presence in the new heaven and the new earth, flowing from the deepest recesses of our hearts. We must quit thinking we can worship God only while doing nothing else. Rather, we can worship Him while doing everything else.

Yet worship isn't the only activity of heaven. We'll also work. Because we're created in the image of God, it should be no surprise that we've been created to work as well. Contrary to what many people believe, work isn't a curse from God as a result of Adam and Eve's sin in the garden. Before the first couple ever took a bite of the forbidden fruit, God gave them the responsibility to work. Although Eden was perfect, it wasn't self-sustaining. God did His part in creating this slice of paradise on earth, but He gave people the responsibility of cultivating it—tilling the soil, planting, and harvesting crops.

Our labor in this fallen world has been burdened by the effects of sin's curse: tired bodies, strained relationships, burdensome corporate and government regulations, and an often chaotic environment. But in the new heaven and the new earth, all of those effects will evaporate because "there will no longer be any curse" (Rev. 22:3). In this world, work—no matter how much we enjoy it—can be exhausting. In the new world, work will be nothing but exhilarating.

Record the blessings of your earthly work.

Record the curses—the negative aspects—of your earthly work.

If your work were made perfect in heaven, what could it look like?

Is there work you dream of being able to do if you weren't restricted by money and opportunity? What would it look like?

If life in the garden of Eden serves as a template of what we can expect in heaven, we can look forward to an eternity of cultivating and creating. In the beginning God created nature and called it good, but He intended His image bearers to cultivate nature—to work and create something very good. For example, cherries are good, but cherry pie is very good; avocados are good, but guacamole is very good; tomatoes and spices are good, but salsa is very good. When God created Adam and placed him in the garden, He commissioned him both to create and to cultivate what God had begun.

Many Scripture use the word *work*. Here are a few:

Whatever you do, do your work heartily, as for the Lord rather than for men.

COLOSSIANS 3:23

Jesus said to them, "My food is to do the will of Him
who sent Me and to accomplish His work."

JOHN 4:34

A Place Called Heaven

It is God who is at work in you, both to
will and to work for His good pleasure.

PHILIPPIANS 2:13

What similarities do you see in the uses of the word *work* in these verses?

How does this biblical understanding of work affect your attitude toward the concept of work today?

How do you see worship and work fitting together on earth even before we reach heaven?

God is the One who plants the desire in our hearts to accomplish His purpose for our lives. One of the best indicators of what we should be doing in this life and what we'll be doing in the next life is the desires that God has placed in our hearts. He doesn't waste gifts, experiences, or desires on us. They're all essential components of our unique purpose—not just in this life but in the life to come as well.

PRAYER

Father God, thank You for giving me a better understanding of worship and work from a heavenly perspective. Thank You for wanting me to create and cultivate from the many resources You've provided here on earth, as well as to prepare for renewed work with You in the kingdom to come. In Christ's name, amen.

DAY 3

ONE JOB DESCRIPTION: RULE & REIGN

God said, "Let Us make man in Our image, according to Our likeness; and let them rule over the fish of the sea and over the birds of the sky and over the cattle and over all the earth, and over every creeping thing that creeps on the earth." God created man in His own image, in the image of God He created him; male and female He created them. God blessed them; and God said to them, "Be fruitful and multiply, and fill the earth, and subdue it; and rule over the fish of the sea and over the birds of the sky and over every living thing that moves on the earth."

GENESIS 1:26-28

One of the many major differences between humankind and the animal and plant world is that God gave Adam and Eve authority and dominion to rule over the earth. The bottom line is that while God rules over the universe and the heavens, He has placed humankind over all the earth.

Just like Adam and Eve, we've been given the abilities and faculties to accomplish this role and responsibility. That's what the phrases "in Our image" (v. 26), "according to Our likeness" (v. 26), and "rule over" (vv. 26,28) mean.

But as we know from Genesis 3, the decision to rebel against God forced Adam and Eve to abdicate their reign over creation. In time God sent "the last Adam," as Paul called Christ in 1 Corinthians 15:45, and established a second Eve—the church—to rule over a new kingdom one day.

When Jesus returns and establishes His thousand-year reign on the earth— a period of time commonly referred to as the millennium—He will appoint His faithful followers to rule with Him. Men and women will be elevated to leadership positions in the new world according to their faithfulness and service to God in the present world.

What was God's original plan for the proper rule over creation?

What are some ways we've drifted from God's original plan for leadership?

Why would God consider what we do in our lives on earth as qualifications for ruling in the new heaven and the new earth?

Our reign will extend beyond the thousand-year rule of Christ during the millennium into the eternal state of the new heaven and the new earth. The final stage of redemption is re-creation, in which we'll be made new and conformed to Christ's purpose for our lives, freed from sin. In heaven we'll still be ourselves but made new. Thus, all the gifts, abilities, and service we have on earth will be very much a part of our lives in heaven.

Many times during His earthly ministry Jesus referred to the idea of being responsible to rule over the resources He gives us. For example:

> *From everyone who has been given much, much will be required;*
> *and to whom they entrusted much, of him they will ask all the more.*

LUKE 12:48

What was Jesus teaching about the responsibility of stewardship or authority over an asset or a gift?

The reward for good work is more work. How has faithfulness to exercise authority in one area of your life led to more responsibility and opportunities in another area?

Two major qualities will be considered for those who will rule in the new heaven and the new earth: godly character and a desire and an ability to rule. We demonstrate these characteristics in the way we live.

What Will We Do in Heaven?

Using His frequent teaching vehicle of the parable, Jesus clearly described a master who gave explicit instructions to his servants and then one day returned unannounced to settle the outcome from his time away:

A nobleman went to a distant country to receive a kingdom for himself, and then return. And he called ten of his slaves, and gave them ten minas and said to them, "Do business with this until I come back." But his citizens hated him and sent a delegation after him, saying, "We do not want this man to reign over us." When he returned, after receiving the kingdom, he ordered that these slaves, to whom he had given the money, be called to him so that he might know what business they had done. The first appeared, saying, "Master, your mina has made ten minas more." And he said to him, "Well done, good slave, because you have been faithful in a very little thing, you are to be in authority over ten cities." The second came, saying, "Your mina, master, has made five minas." And he said to him also, "And you are to be over five cities." Another came, saying, "Master, here is your mina, which I kept put away in a handkerchief; for I was afraid of you, because you are an exacting man; you take up what you did not lay down and reap what you did not sow." He said to him, "By your own words I will judge you, you worthless slave. Did you know that I am an exacting man, taking up what I did not lay down and reaping what I did not sow? Then why did you not put my money in the bank, and having come, I would have collected it with interest?" Then he said to the bystanders, "Take the mina away from him and give it to the one who has the ten minas." And they said to him, "Master, he has ten minas already." I tell you that to everyone who has, more shall be given, but from the one who does not have, even what he does have shall be taken away. But these enemies of mine, who did not want me to reign over them, bring them here and slay them in my presence.

LUKE 19:12-27

How did the obedience and initiative of the servants in the absence of the master matter at the time of his return?

How did the attitude of the man left with one mina affect his future with the master? Why?

What does this parable teach us about God's priorities?

How could you use your time, talents, and treasure to build the kingdom of God? Respond on the chart.

Time, Talents, Treasure	Building the Kingdom

God has placed in our hands not only the precious gift of our lives but also a great responsibility to use our limited time, talents, and treasure in this life to further His kingdom rather our own. As we obey, He will prepare us for the time in eternity when we'll rule and reign with Him.

PRAYER

King Jesus, it's humbling to consider that You'll allow me the opportunity to return to the days of the garden, ruling and reigning as You originally desired for me to do. May I be like the servant with ten minas, found faithful until the day of Your return. In Your name, amen.

DAY 4
JUDGING & GOVERNING, RULING & REIGNING

Ruling and reigning with Christ in His new kingdom will involve at least two responsibilities: judging and governing. Our current world system demonstrates the difference between these two roles. Judging deals with the application of the law in people's lives. Governing is the administration not only of laws but also of policies and politics.

Paul wrote, "The saints will judge the world" (1 Cor. 6:2). The word translated *judge* can refer to pronouncing a verdict against someone, but it can also be a synonym for *govern*. As corulers with Jesus Christ, we'll be responsible for both judging and governing in His new kingdom. Although there's no indication in Scripture that Christians will pronounce judgments against other human beings, we very well could be involved in the future judgment of certain angels.

In the next verse Paul asked, "Do you not know that we will judge angels?" (v. 3). This is a curious question since Psalm 8:4-5 says God made humans lower than angels (NIV). But in the eternal state our positions will be reversed; we'll be elevated higher than angels. The word Paul used for *judge* means "to pass judgment based on various factors." This term implies a level of responsibility. Or Paul could have used *judge* as a synonym for our ruling over the angelic orders in the new heaven and the new earth. The point is that believers will bear the responsibility of judging in heaven.

Why might many Christians struggle with the thought of judging and governing in heaven?

What are some ways our twenty-first-century political system has distorted the idea that any governing body could be righteous and godly?

101

A Place Called Heaven

In the days of the Bible, kings appointed faithful, responsible citizens as coregents over areas of their kingdoms. To better understand the biblical paradigm of governing and ruling, let's look at two of those situations in the Bible.

JOSEPH

Pharaoh said to his servants, "Can we find a man like this, in whom is a divine spirit?" So Pharaoh said to Joseph, "Since God has informed you of all this, there is no one so discerning and wise as you are. You shall be over my house, and according to your command all my people shall do homage; only in the throne I will be greater than you." Pharaoh said to Joseph, "See, I have set you over all the land of Egypt." Then Pharaoh took off his signet ring from his hand and put it on Joseph's hand, and clothed him in garments of fine linen and put the gold necklace around his neck. He had him ride in his second chariot; and they proclaimed before him, "Bow the knee!" And he set him over all the land of Egypt. Moreover, Pharaoh said to Joseph, "Though I am Pharaoh, yet without your permission no one shall raise his hand or foot in all the land of Egypt."

GENESIS 41:38-44

List the qualities Pharaoh saw in Joseph that led him to grant authority to Joseph.

Where did Joseph's authority truly come from? How does this source relate to the authority that God has given believers to judge and govern?

Pharaoh gave Joseph all authority over the land of Egypt. His faithfulness and display of spiritual wisdom became unmistakably obvious. After receiving the call from Pharaoh, Joseph used his discernment and wisdom to judge and govern all of Egypt. In a similar way, Jesus has given all Christians authority to act in His name (see Matt. 28:18-20). From His example we learn how to exercise godly authority in carrying out the work of His kingdom.

DANIEL

King Nebuchadnezzar fell on his face and did homage to Daniel, and gave orders to present to him an offering and fragrant incense. The king answered Daniel and said, "Surely your God is a God of gods and a Lord of kings and a revealer of mysteries, since you have been able to reveal this mystery." Then the king promoted Daniel and gave him many great gifts, and he made him ruler over the whole province of Babylon and chief prefect over all the wise men of Babylon. And Daniel made request of the king, and he appointed Shadrach, Meshach and Abed-nego over the administration of the province of Babylon, while Daniel was at the king's court.

DANIEL 2:46-49

It seemed good to Darius to appoint 120 satraps over the kingdom, that they would be in charge of the whole kingdom, and over them three commissioners (of whom Daniel was one), that these satraps might be accountable to them, and that the king might not suffer loss. Then this Daniel began distinguishing himself among the commissioners and satraps because he possessed an extraordinary spirit, and the king planned to appoint him over the entire kingdom.

DANIEL 6:1-3

What leadership qualities do you see in Daniel's life?

Following Daniel's detailed interpretation of the king's dream, Nebuchadnezzar acknowledged both Daniel's leadership and God's authority. What do you think motivated the king to further promote Daniel over the entire province?

How has God maximized your gifts for His glory? How are you using your gifts now?

A Place Called Heaven

We live in a day when many people strive for titles without a testimony that warrants the authority they desire. In these Old Testament examples we see the exact opposite; these men had proved their blessing from God and their favor from men by their wisdom, courage, and integrity before they were offered promotions. Each one proved he was worthy of governing before receiving his title.

Although Scripture provides few details about what ruling in God's new kingdom will entail, we can be confident that the experience will be exhilarating and eternally fulfilling, especially in light of being a reward for faithfulness to the Lord in this life.

God assigned Adam and Eve to reign over the Lord's creation in the garden. In the same way, God will reward believers with leadership responsibilities in heaven, reigning over the Lord's new creation.

In what ways do you enjoy leadership and influence now? How do these responsibilities help you understand the role you'll fulfill in heaven?

PRAYER

Father God, although there are many aspects of ruling and governing I don't completely understand, I trust You to provide for me in heaven just as You do here. I know that if I'm under Your authority in heaven, I'll be exactly where I need to be, doing exactly what I should be doing. Thank You that I can always trust You. In Christ's name, amen.

THREE PERKS OF HEAVEN

This week we've explored our worship and work in heaven. Today we'll outline three additional activities we can look forward to.

ENJOYING OTHER BELIEVERS

God Himself is a community—Father, Son, and Holy Spirit. Therefore, He created people for community as well. We're wired for interaction with Him and one another. This quality will only become more pronounced in heaven because there will be no sin to corrupt our relationships. In fact, in a perfect atmosphere we'll finally experience the most fulfilling, intimate connections we've ever known. We'll encounter flawless fellowship with everyone in heaven.

In heaven we'll experience perfect unity, peace, love, acceptance, security, loyalty, faithfulness, and every other positive relational quality imaginable. Gone forever will be gossip, apathy, infidelity, jealousy, insecurity, bitterness, pettiness, and hate.

Beside each statement record the name of at least one person who has gone to heaven.

The Christian family member you miss most:

The Christian friend you miss most:

A well-known Christian pastor, author, scientist, artist, or athlete:

A person in the Bible you've always wanted to meet:

LEARNING MORE ABOUT GOD

In the new heaven and the new earth we'll understand more about God than we do now. But exactly how will that knowledge come? At the moment of our death and entrance into God's presence, will the Lord instantaneously download into our minds a perfect, complete understanding of Himself? Maybe.

But think about your most valued relationships on earth—your mate, your children, your closest friends. No doubt you've discovered the joy of incrementally learning more about them through the years rather than experiencing an information dump all at once. Imagine how boring eternity would be if we instantly knew everything about God and had nothing new to discover throughout eternity.

Paul explained:

> *We know in part and we prophesy in part; but when the perfect comes, the partial will be done away. When I was a child, I used to speak like a child, think like a child, reason like a child; when I became a man, I did away with childish things. For now we see in a mirror dimly, but then face to face; now I know in part, but then I will know fully just as I also have been fully known.*
>
> 1 CORINTHIANS 13:9-12

Paul stated that on earth, even though we live in a relationship with Christ, our view of God is like looking at a dimly lit mirror or through a dark glass. The image isn't bright and clear. We know an image is there, but the details are sketchy. Full, complete knowledge isn't yet possible. But our face-to-face view in heaven will allow us the opportunity to fully know Christ in all His glory.

Have you ever realized that in heaven you'll learn about God forever? Why should this prospect fill believers with longing and anticipation?

EXPERIENCING TRUE REST

Although there will be continual activity in heaven in the forms of worship and work, there will also be rest. We know that on the seventh day following creation, God Himself rested (see Gen. 2:2). This doesn't mean that He was exhausted but that He desired to reserve time to reflect on and enjoy what He had created. God commanded His people to follow this same pattern every Sabbath (see Ex. 20:8). He also designated resting periods in other seasons as well.

As busy Americans, we spend a lot of money on material possessions for leisure but rarely or never take time to enjoy them. Although physical rest is vitally important, mental, emotional, and spiritual rest also have great value.

John wrote:

> *I heard a voice from heaven, saying, "Write, 'Blessed are the dead who die in the Lord from now on!' " "Yes," says the Spirit, "so that they may rest from their labors, for their deeds follow with them."*
>
> REVELATION 14:13

This verse means that in heaven believers will finally be freed and released from the burden and struggle of living a godly lifestyle in a broken, fallen world. Hostility and persecution will be things of the past.

What's one burden you'll be glad to lay down at the feet of the risen Christ?

How can offering people rest in heaven influence our evangelistic conversations?

PRAYER

Heavenly Father, thank You for the community I'll experience in heaven, with unity and perfection being the focus of all. Thank You for the opportunity not only to be in Your presence but also to know You more fully. Thank You for Your promise of rest for my soul. In Christ's name, amen.

Who Will Be in Heaven?

Start

As we get started, share one truth about heaven you learned during the first four weeks of study that may have surprised you.

In your lifetime you've likely heard a lot of people say that a deceased person is looking down on them from heaven. But on what do they base their belief that this person is in heaven? Many people believe people get to heaven by doing more good than bad. Others see heaven as a generic place where people who leave us reside. However, Scripture always treats heaven as a specific place we can go to only if we place our faith in Jesus. The gospel of Jesus Christ is the road map to heaven.

Whom are you most looking forward to seeing in heaven? Why?

Before we watch Dr. Jeffress's teaching, would someone open with prayer, asking God to teach us what He wants us to know about heaven?

Watch

Use these statements to follow along as you watch video session 5.

Many will be surprised who thought God will welcome them into heaven, but in fact, God will turn them away.

The journey to heaven or hell begins in this life.

Signposts That Lead to Heaven

1. We have to acknowledge that we have a sin problem.

   Eternal death is the separation of our spirit from God.

2. God is sinless.

   The truth that you and I can overlook sin in other people and in our lives is not because we are so like God; it's because we are so unlike God.

   God has a zero tolerance level for sin because He is wholly sinless.

3. Jesus is the solution to our sin problem.

   When Jesus died on the cross, He took all of the punishment from God that you and I deserve.

   Jesus was the only one qualified to bear the punishment we deserve, and He is the only person in history who had enough righteousness to get to heaven.

4. We must choose to accept Christ's offer of forgiveness.

Video sessions available at LifeWay.com/APlaceCalledHeaven

Discuss

Discuss the video with the group, using the questions below.

Why do you think our culture struggles so much with the claim that Jesus is the only way to heaven?

Have you ever met any resistance to your belief that Jesus is the only way to heaven?

Why did Dr. Jeffress say we might be surprised by who's in heaven and who isn't?

Dr. Jeffress said about some people who consider themselves believers, "It doesn't matter how sincere you are; you can be sincerely wrong." What did he mean?

Why are so many people reluctant to admit they're sinners? Why is that a difficult confession, even though we all know in our hearts that it's true?

We often place human parameters on God, denying His holiness and foolishly believing we know best. Why must we enter heaven by the means God has prescribed?

How do most of us choose the sins we'll tolerate and those we won't?

Why is Jesus the answer to every problem with sin that we experience?

What are some ways we struggle to receive all God has given us through His righteousness? Why is such an amazing gift hard to accept?

Read Romans 10:13. What are some ways we might struggle with the teaching that whoever calls on the name of the Lord can be saved, even a serial killer like Westley Allan Dodd?

Read week 5 and complete the activities before the next group session.

Who Will Be in Heaven?

Maps can be useful in navigating unfamiliar territory. Unfortunately, I had to learn the value of maps the hard way some years ago. A pastor friend had invited me to Canada to speak at his church's Valentine's banquet. I departed from Dallas early one morning and, after changing planes in Minneapolis, landed in Winnipeg, Manitoba, around four p.m. with plenty of time to spare.

After retrieving my luggage, I stood out front waiting for my host to arrive … and waiting … and waiting. After about thirty minutes I strolled back inside the terminal to call the pastor's home. When I looked down at the invitation letter he had mailed a few weeks earlier to retrieve his phone number, I notice that the city and province on his letterhead didn't correspond to my present location. Because I had preached for the pastor in Winnipeg ten years earlier, I had assumed he was still at the same church. Big mistake.

Accidentally traveling to the wrong location can be embarrassing. But there's one time in your life when you don't want to arrive at the wrong destination—the day of your death. We may be surprised to find who'll be in heaven. Some people we think will be in heaven won't be there, while many people we don't think should be there will be. The worst surprise of all will be for those who assumed they would be welcomed into God's presence but instead will be turned away.

When I suggest that those who are in heaven may surprise us, I'm not implying we'll see Hindus, Buddhists, and Muslims standing alongside Christians. I'm saying because only God is able "to judge the thoughts and intentions of the heart" (Heb. 4:12), He alone knows who has sincerely placed his or her faith in Christ for the forgiveness of sins. You may be truly surprised by others who are or aren't in heaven. But hopefully, you won't be surprised about your own eternal fate.

DAY 1
THE ROAD TO HEAVEN

Lots of people believe lots of different things about how to get to heaven, but all people can't be right. This week's personal studies will help us capture a clear picture of the road to heaven.

Why do so many people of all religions espouse the idea that all roads lead to heaven? Do you think people genuinely believe this? Explain.

Why do so many people want to put all religions and spiritual leaders on the same spiritual plane? Where have you seen examples of this effort?

In your experience, how do unbelieving people think they get to heaven?

Savor once again these well-known verses about God's love:

> *God so loved the world, that He gave His only begotten Son,*
> *that whoever believes in Him shall not perish, but have eternal*
> *life. For God did not send the Son into the world to judge*
> *the world, but that the world might be saved through Him.*

JOHN 3:16-17

Even most non-Christians have no issue with these verses because they focus on God's great love and express His desire not to judge people but to save them. But a few chapters later Jesus made an incendiary claim that catches many people dead in their tracks because it doesn't fit into their idea of a wide road to heaven:

A Place Called Heaven

Jesus said to him, "I am the way, and the truth, and
the life; no one comes to the Father but through Me."

In our diverse and choice-crazed culture, claiming that there's only one way to heaven provokes a riot these days. Suddenly God's love and desire to save are overshadowed by a restrictive qualification.

The Bible clearly says only people who've trusted in Christ for the forgiveness of their sins will reside in the new heaven and the new earth. When people argue against the exclusivity of Christ for salvation by saying, "No one but God can decide who will be in heaven," they miss a crucial truth: God has already decided the standard by which people will be admitted into His presence. When we declare that faith in Christ offers the only path to heaven, we aren't creating our own criterion but simply articulating the requirement God established.

Why do you suppose our culture has become so consumed with the concept of love while losing the standards and accountability that come with true love?

How does the truth of John 3:16 depend on the reality of John 14:6?

Why do so many people see John 14:6 as a limitation rather than a gift?

All people can rely on Scripture to shine a light on the way to heaven:

The word of God is living and active and sharper than any two-edged
sword, and piercing as far as the division of soul and spirit, of both joints
and marrow, and able to judge the thoughts and intentions of the heart.

HEBREWS 4:12

Why do we need to look to Scripture to find the one true revelation of the road to heaven?

What must people discount about Scripture to arrive at the conclusion that all roads lead to heaven?

We can be certain there's a road to heaven because Scripture has revealed it to us. It isn't obscure or hard to find. In fact, it's the central message in all of Scripture. When we approach God's Word, it reveals the thoughts and intentions of our hearts and directs us down the right path. This is why we must rely on the teachings of Scripture to reveal the road to heaven. It's a constant, never-changing path. While culture and opinions change, the road to heaven is always the same:

> *Jesus Christ is the same yesterday and today and forever.*
> *Do not be carried away by varied and strange teachings.*
>
> HEBREWS 13:8-9

We often see Hebrews 13:8 quoted alone, but reading it in context with verse 9 brings a broader meaning to a discussion of what's required to enter heaven. In fact, we could state the meaning of the author of Hebrews this way: "Jesus Christ is the same yesterday and today and forever, [so] do not be carried away by varied and strange teachings." Or we could say, "Do not be carried away by varied and strange teachings, [because] Jesus Christ is the same yesterday and today and forever."

How does the truth of Hebrews 13:8 support the stability and accuracy of your faith?

If you're a seeker—someone who's interested in Christianity—or if you've been inactive in the faith for some time, possibly having attended church as a child but now seeking truth as an adult, a review of the gospel of Jesus Christ is always a good idea, whether you've been a Christian for six months or sixty years. In the remaining personal studies this week, we'll look at components of the gospel message as signposts directing us to heaven.

> Record your understanding of the gospel message succinctly enough that you could share it with someone during an elevator ride. We'll come back and evaluate what you've written at the end of the week.

PRAYER

Father God, thank You for giving the gospel message that saves souls and allows me to see that Jesus Christ is the way, the truth, and the life. Help me realize the truth and weight of that statement each day as I seek to honor and glorify Your name.

DAY 2

SIGNPOST 1:
WE HAVE A SIN PROBLEM

No one accidentally ends up in heaven or hell without warning. Instead, there are definite signposts along the way that alert us as to whether we're on the right path leading to the right destination. The journey to heaven or hell begins in our earthly lives. If we're truly on the road that leads to heaven, we must acknowledge four signposts along the way. Over the next few days we'll take a look at those signposts.

Many people refuse to go beyond this point. They would rather turn around and go in another direction than face the unsettling truth, but here's the undeniable reality about every human being:

> *There is none righteous, not even one;*
> *There is none who understands,*
> *There is none who seeks for God;*
> *All have turned aside, together they have become useless;*
> *There is none who does good,*
> *There is not even one.*

ROMANS 3:10-12

Why is it often difficult for us to acknowledge our sin?

How would the unbelieving people you know define the word *righteous?*

To be righteous means to be in right standing with God. And how many people are naturally in a right relationship with God? Zilch, zero, *nada*—or as Paul said, "There is none righteous, not even one" (v. 10). We're all sinners. Admittedly, we can always point to people who are worse than we are, such as drug dealers, murderers, and child pornographers. We may not be as bad as we could be, but we're just as bad off as we can be. All of us have sinned, creating an eternal gulf between God and ourselves.

The sin we inherited from Adam infects every action, every motive, and every thought. In our honest moments we know that's true. Have you ever been minding your own business—maybe even sitting in church—when a horrible thought came into your mind? *Where did that come from?* you wonder. It's a symptom of the sickness we've all contracted.

Where does your desire for sin most often show up in your daily life?

Although people aren't righteous, most seek to be righteous even if they would never use that word. How do the people around you seek to make themselves right with God?

What are some ways even followers of Jesus try to make themselves right with God through their work instead of trusting in Jesus?

Generally, most people consider themselves good people. They believe that they're doing their best and that only really bad people are sinners. The Bible tells a different story. The testimony of Scripture is that all of us are sinners and that sin consistently reveals itself in our lives.

We experience the symptoms of sin every day, yet some people still want to claim that they're innocent—that the label *sinner* doesn't apply to them. These people are like an only child who, while throwing a baseball in the house, breaks his mother's lamp. When she asks him about it, he claims he was playing catch with Fred, his imaginary friend, and Fred threw the ball into the lamp.

Scripture is clear:

> *If we say that we have no sin, we are deceiving ourselves*
> *and the truth is not in us. If we say that we have not sinned,*
> *we make Him a liar and His word is not in us.*

1 JOHN 1:8,10

118

Why does denying that we are sinners make God a liar?

When are you most tempted to deny your sinfulness? Why is truly denying your sin impossible?

Why do we try to minimize our sinfulness?

When things go wrong—like broken lamps—it's our natural tendency to blame someone else. God, who's perfectly righteous, has declared that we're all sinners. He has already rendered His verdict on our lives through His Word.

When we deny our sin, we're pointing away from all the evidence to the contrary. We claim our innocence while all the evidence points to our guilt. But as the apostle John declared, when we deny our sin , we call God a liar because we're rejecting all the rock-solid evidence God has amassed in His case against us. We've all sinned, and that sin has earned us death:

> *The wages of sin is death.*
> ROMANS 6:23

When Paul wrote that sin results in death, he meant spiritual death. What's the difference between physical and spiritual death?

Whether or not we acknowledge it, the fact remains that we're all sinners. And the result of sin is death. The Greek word translated *death* literally means "separation." Just as physical death is the separation of our body from our spirit, spiritual death is the separation of our spirit from God. Physical death is temporary, but spiritual death is eternal. Death is God's righteous judgment on sin. Our sin is a problem because it has caused separation between us and God. Because He's sinless, He can't abide our sin. We'll talk more about that signpost in day 3.

Use the chart below to express ways sin has caused separation in your relationships.

Relationship	Ways Sin Has Caused Separation
God	
Other people	
The world around you	

PRAYER

Father God, I confess that my sin has resulted in separation in my relationships with You, with others, and with the world around me. Today I'm thankful for Your grace and mercy to me despite all my sin. I thank You for extending life and grace to me although I deserved death. In Christ's name, amen.

DAY 3
SIGNPOST 2:
GOD IS SINLESS

I used to tell my teenage girls, "My house, my rules." Because God is the Creator of heaven, He gets to create the rules. And the standing rule of heaven is holiness. God's standard demands absolute perfection. In Scripture God repeatedly commands us to be holy (see Lev. 11:44-45; 19:2; 20:7; 1 Pet. 1:16).

Define the word *holy*.

What does it mean for God to be holy?

Holiness is absolute perfection. The word means "separate." The problem is, as we've already discovered this week, we're not holy, and God is. This reality compounds the problem of sin because it separates us from God. So how can a sin-infected person ever relate to a sinless God? "Well, God can overlook our imperfection, can't He?" many people ask. "After all, shouldn't God be as tolerant of our sin as we are of other people's sins?" Unfortunately (or fortunately), God isn't like us. The prophet Habakkuk wrote about God:

> *Your eyes are too pure to approve evil,*
> *And You can not look on wickedness with favor.*

HABAKKUK 1:13

How does this signpost on the road to heaven help us realize our desperate need for God?

A Place Called Heaven

Have you ever doubted God's holiness? If so, why?

When you couple the reality of this second signpost about God's holiness with the truth of the first signpost about our sinfulness, you can get discouraged very quickly. For example, imagine you're making a trip from Oklahoma to Winnipeg, Manitoba, Canada, and you see a sign that says, "Winnipeg, 1,300 miles." It's a long trip, but with perseverance you can make it—until you notice your gas gauge indicates only a quarter of a tank left. No problem. You pull into a gas station, only to discover that you have no cash or credit cards with you. There's a serious deficit between what you have and what you need to reach your destination. At this point you seriously consider doing a U-turn because you see no answer to your dilemma.

When do you first remember being confronted with the holiness of God? How did you respond?

Do you give much thought to God's holiness in your daily life? Why or why not?

Peter admonished believers to be holy like God:

> *As obedient children, do not be conformed to the former lusts*
> *which were yours in your ignorance, but like the Holy One*
> *who called you, be holy yourselves also in all your behavior;*
> *because it is written, "You shall be holy, for I am holy."*
>
> 1 PETER 1:14-16

Why does God's holiness present a problem for us?

The Bible says if we're to make it to heaven, our spiritual tank needs to be filled with perfection. The only problem is that none of us can do enough good things to get to heaven. While some people may think of themselves as better than others, the truth is that even our good acts aren't enough (see Isa. 64:6). God demands that our spiritual gas tanks be full and running over if we're going to make it into His presence. We have no righteousness apart from Christ.

Signpost 1 warned us to acknowledge that we're sinful and unholy. Signpost 2 tells us that God is holy. His character and works are perfect, making Him an incredible God for unholy people. Our sinfulness and God's holiness lead us to signpost 3—our need for a Savior.

Make a list of the attributes or characteristics of God that cause you to worship Him.

PRAYER

Lord God, I'm thankful that You aren't like me. I praise You for Your absolute moral perfection. You've never had a wrong thought, and You've never done a bad deed. All You are and all You do are perfect. Thank You for sending Jesus as the perfect, righteous substitute for my sin. In Christ's name, amen.

DAY 4
SIGNPOST 3:
WE NEED A SAVIOR

This week we've used the analogy of a trip to think about our journey to heaven. Signposts 1 and 2 led us to realize that we're completely out of gas and that no amount of work on our part can take us there. We can't fill our own tanks with the holiness we need to make it to heaven on our own. However, imagine that out of nowhere a huge gasoline tanker appears and stops along the rode beside you. The driver asks, "What's the problem?" You explain that you ran out of gas. He grins, points to his rig, and says, "I have more gas in this tanker than you could ever need in your little car. May I fill your tank for you?"

> What's the most sacrificial thing someone has ever done for you? What depth of gratitude did you feel for the person who helped you?

> What's the nicest thing you've ever done for someone else, expecting nothing in return?

When Jesus Christ died on the cross for our sins, two amazing transactions took place.

1. Jesus—the perfect Son of God who had never sinned—voluntarily accepted the punishment from God that we deserve for our sins. Because God is holy, He couldn't simply overlook or decide not to punish our sins. Someone had to pay for our sin, and Jesus volunteered to do that.
2. The second transaction on the cross was even more amazing. God credited us with the righteousness—or perfection—of Jesus. Even though we don't have enough goodness to make it to heaven on our own, Jesus has more than enough and is willing to give us all we need to make up for our deficit. The apostle Paul described these two transactions—Christ's being credited for our sin and our being credited for His righteousness:

Who Will Be in Heaven?

He made Him who knew no sin to be sin on our behalf,
so that we might become the righteousness of God in Him.

2 CORINTHIANS 5:21

What made Jesus the only person qualified to provide a sacrifice for our sins?
What made Him unique?

If Jesus was the only person qualified, why do we often try to save
ourselves and others?

Jesus was the only person qualified to bear the punishment for our sins and offer us
complete perfection because He was uniquely different from any other person who
ever walked on this planet. In fact, in John 3:16 "only begotten Son" could have
been translated "unique Son." He alone is the Son of God. The signpost declaring
Jesus to be our sin substitute is the one that causes many people to stop, stumble,
and begin searching for an alternative road to heaven.

What alternative paths to heaven do the people around you seek?

Even if people sincerely believe these paths will take them to heaven,
why are they ultimately misguided?

Many sincere, well-meaning, and faithful followers of other religions—such as
Buddhists, Hindus, Muslims, Jehovah's Witnesses, and Mormons—believe Jesus
was a good man, a holy man, and a wise man pointing the way to either enlighten-
ment or heaven. But none of them believe His claims to divinity and exclusivity
as the only means of salvation and as the only way to heaven.

C. S. Lewis called such a denial foolish:

> I am trying here to prevent anyone saying the really foolish thing that people often say about Him: "I'm ready to accept Jesus as a great moral teacher, but I don't accept His claim to be God." That is the one thing we must not say. A man who was merely a man and said the sort of things Jesus said would not be a great moral teacher. He would either be a lunatic—on a level with the man who says he is a poached egg—or else he would be the Devil of Hell. You must make your choice. Either this man was, and is, the Son of God: or else a madman or something worse. You can shut Him up for a fool, you can spit on Him and kill Him as a demon; or you can fall at His feet and call Him Lord and God. But let us not come with any patronizing nonsense about His being a great human teacher. He has not left that open to us. He did not intend to.[1]

We must either embrace Jesus' claim that He's God's Son, or we must reject it. There's no intellectually honest alternative, given Jesus' claim that He's the only solution to bridge the gap between our sinfulness and God's holiness. Paul wrote:

> *There is one God, and one mediator also*
> *between God and men, the man Christ Jesus.*
>
> 1 TIMOTHY 2:5

Because of the two transactions that took place on the cross—Christ's receiving the punishment we deserve and our receiving the righteousness we don't deserve—God offers us entrance into heaven. We must have a mediator to plead our case before God. The mediation we need happens through faith in Christ. Paul explained it this way:

> *Having been justified by faith, we have peace*
> *with God through our Lord Jesus Christ.*
>
> ROMANS 5:1

The word *justified* means we're absolved of sin. Justification doesn't make us righteous in the sense that we'll never sin again. Rather, justification declares us righteous, as when a judge issues a pardon to a guilty criminal. This type of pardon can come only from Christ.

Although we've been "justified by faith," we try to justify ourselves all the time. Why do even believers in Jesus try to bridge the gap between our sin and God's holiness?

Because Jesus took our sins on Himself and paid for them on the cross, God forgives us and proclaims us pardoned. The pardon comes from Christ's forgiveness. Only forgiveness, never our works of righteousness, can bridge the gap between us and God. A recognition that only Jesus can forgive our sins leads to the final signpost on the road to heaven: we must accept His offer of forgiveness.

When did you first realize that all your works of righteousness weren't enough? What was that realization like?

Whom do you know who might be in the process of coming to that same realization? Take a moment to pray for them.

PRAYER

Gracious Jesus, thank You for being all I need. You're the perfect, sinless Savior who overcame my sin with Your righteousness and bridged the gap between me and God. Thank You for doing all that was necessary for me to know God. In Your name, amen.

1. C. S. Lewis, *Mere Christianity* (New York: HarperOne, 1980), 52.

DAY 5

SIGNPOST 4:
ACCEPT CHRIST'S
OFFER OF FORGIVENESS

When has someone offered you forgiveness even though you were totally undeserving of forgiveness? What did that offer mean to you?

If you've made it this far on the narrow road that leads to heaven, you're closer than the vast majority of people who've ever lived. When some people encounter messages declaring that they're guilty before God and deserve His punishment, they repent, accept Christ's forgiveness for their sin, and confess Him as their Lord and Savior. Others who are willing to admit their mistakes still can't accept the idea that Jesus Christ is the only solution to their need for God's forgiveness, and they start looking for a different path.

Amazingly, some people agree that they're sinners who deserve punishment, that God is holy and demands complete perfection, and that Jesus is the only solution to their need for God's forgiveness. Yet they stop where they are and fail to travel a few steps further to embrace the truth that they must choose to accept Christ's offer of forgiveness.

Why must we make the active choice to accept the offer of forgiveness? Why isn't simply acknowledging the offer enough?

Think back for a moment to the driver of the gas truck who offers to fill your empty tank so that you can make it to your destination. You have a need (gas), and he has the provision for your need (lots of gas). Intellectually agreeing with both of those realities doesn't put one drop of gasoline into your empty tank. You must unscrew the cap on your empty gas tank and receive the gift of the fuel you desperately need.

There has to be a point in time when by faith you acknowledge your need for God's forgiveness, accept Christ's payment for your sins, and allow Him to fill you with His perfection. God doesn't force anyone to receive His offer of forgiveness. Only those who choose to receive His gift will be granted entry into heaven:

> *If you confess with your mouth Jesus as Lord, and believe in your heart that God raised Him from the dead, you will be saved. For the Scripture says, "Whoever believes in Him will not be disappointed." For there is no distinction between Jew and Greek; for the same Lord is Lord of all, abounding in riches for all who call on Him; for "Whoever will call on the name of the Lord will be saved."*

ROMANS 10:9,11-13

According to these verses, what must a person do to accept Christ's offer of forgiveness?

Why is it important to realize that Jesus forgives without qualification or distinction—that His offer is for everyone?

Accepting Christ's offer of forgiveness means confessing your sins and believing in His sacrifice on your behalf: "Whoever will call on the name of the Lord will be saved" (v. 13). God doesn't care what kind of life you've lived. He doesn't care whether you've been in church every time the doors were open or whether you've never been inside a church building in your life. All people need forgiveness and can find it in Jesus Christ. His grace is unconditional. His forgiveness is a call to action:

> *How then will they call on Him in whom they have not believed? How will they believe in Him whom they have not heard? And how will they hear without a preacher?*

ROMANS 10:14

Why should the forgiveness we've received from Jesus lead us to tell other people about His forgiveness?

A Place Called Heaven

Why isn't telling others how to get to heaven just the task of professional ministers and preachers?

Don't let the word *preacher* in this verse mislead you. Paul was calling for all believers in Jesus to take the gospel and communicate it to other people who haven't yet believed. Lost people can't accept Jesus' offer of forgiveness unless they hear about His offer of forgiveness. For that to happen, believers must tell them about Jesus. Being on the road to a place called heaven means we consistently invite people to join us on our journey.

Record the names of three people who aren't on the road to heaven. Take time to pray for them this week.

1.

2.

3.

Has there ever been a time when you accepted Christ's offer of forgiveness? If not, what's keep you from accepting the offer? If so, what has changed about your life since that time?

This might be a good time to pause and ask where you are on the road to heaven. Perhaps you're ready and willing to open your heart to receive God's offer of forgiveness so that you'll be sure God will welcome you into His presence someday. The prayer that closes today's study can serve two purposes.

1. If you've never received Jesus Christ into your life for salvation, pray the prayer or a similar one that expresses your desire for forgiveness. If that prayer represents the desire of your heart, you can be assured that you're on the road that leads to heaven. If you prayed a prayer like this for the first time, tell someone—a friend, a pastor, or someone who's completing this study with you.
2. If you know people who may be on the road to hell, pray that God will use you to show them His way, His truth, and His life. When the right time comes, lead them to pray this prayer of repentance and forgiveness.

PRAYER

Thank You, Father, for loving me. I realize that I've failed You in many ways, and I'm truly sorry for the sin in my life. But I believe You loved me so much that You sent Your Son, Jesus, to die on the cross for me. I believe Jesus took the punishment I deserve for my sins. So right now I'm trusting in what Jesus did for me—not my own good works— to save me from my sins. Thank You for forgiving me and allowing me to spend the rest of my life serving You. In Christ's name, amen.

WEEK

6

How Can We
Prepare for Our
Journey to Heaven?

Start

Last week's material was filled with many great truths about the journey to heaven.

Based on all you've learned in this Bible study, what do you expect heaven to be like?

What's one feature of heaven you're looking forward to?

It doesn't matter how many Scriptures you've read, how many sermons you've heard, or how many facts about eternity you understand if you discover that you aren't ready to experience heaven. Being prepared for heaven is the primary goal.

Regardless of how much you may know about the gospel or how many years you've been a Christian, this final week of study will provide you with more to consider about heaven and new ways to deepen your faith as you anticipate your future in eternity. If you've decided at any point during this study that you don't yet know Jesus Christ as your personal Lord and Savior, this will be the time to place your faith in Him.

Before we watch Dr. Jeffress's teaching, would someone open with prayer, asking God to help us be prepared for a place called heaven?

Watch

Use these statements to follow along as you watch video session 6.

The only way we can escape God's eternal judgment is by trusting in Christ as our Savior now before we die.

The judgment for Christians is called the judgment seat of Christ. It results not in condemnation but in God's commendation for the lives we have lived for Christ.

Justified means "to declare to be righteous."

Every sin we commit against God only adds to the debt we owe God. If we die while we're still in that spiritual deficit with God, we spend eternity separated from Him.

When you become a Christian, God no longer sees your sin. He sees the righteousness of His Son, Jesus Christ.

God's justification exempts us from God's condemnation, but it doesn't exempt us from God's evaluation of our life.

We've got to distinguish between the value of our works before we are saved and the value of our works after we are saved.

While our works are worthless in securing us a place in heaven, they are integral in determining our experience in heaven.

Before we are saved, our works are sufficient to condemn us before God, but after we are saved, our good works are sufficient to commend us to God.

Is your life going to be judged as having substance, of being invested in growing God's kingdom, or will your life be judged as being inconsequential?

The judgment seat of Christ is going to be an honest evaluation of everything we've done, whether it is good—lasting, eternal—or worthless.

Video sessions available at LifeWay.com/APlaceCalledHeaven

Discuss

Discuss the video with the group, using the questions below.

Why does the idea of God's judgment terrify most people—Christian or not?

Why is it crucial for Christians to fully understand the nature of both types of judgment Dr. Jeffress described—the great white throne judgment and the judgment seat of Christ?

Why is it so difficult for even Christians to accept that after trusting Christ, there's no condemnation of our lives?

Why did Dr. Jeffress, a pastor, say that laypeople have a better opportunity to secure rewards in heaven than those like himself in vocational ministry?

How can the judgment seat of Christ become a positive, inspiring motivator for the way we live the rest of our lives?

Read Romans 5:1. Based on this verse, what benefits do we receive from trusting in Christ?

If Christ has fully paid the debt for sin, why do so many of us live under the burden of sin?

Why do we tend to stay focused on our own lives even though we realize that heaven is at stake for others around us?

Discuss Jesus' words in Luke 8:17: "Nothing is hidden that will not become evident, nor anything secret that will not be known and come to light." Why should His statement motivate us to do good works?

Read week 6 and complete the activities to conclude this Bible study.

How Can We Prepare for Our Journey to Heaven?

We began this Bible study by thinking about preparations we would make for a journey to a distant country. We talked about all the matters that would need to be attended to before we left in order to ensure a successful journey. Now that we've reached our final week of study, I hope you feel more prepared for your trip to a place called heaven.

Because we don't know when we'll suddenly be called away to heaven, we have to learn how to fulfill our responsibilities in this world while preparing for the next world. Our true country is heaven; it's where our true citizenship lies. Paul wrote:

> *We are citizens of heaven, where the Lord Jesus Christ lives.*
> *And we are eagerly waiting for him to return as our Savior.*
>
> PHILIPPIANS 3:20, NLT

Yet God has charged each of us with responsibilities in this world that include our work, our families, and especially our ministry for Him as "ambassadors for Christ" (2 Cor 5:20). As Christians, although we'll soon depart for our eternal home, we have God-given assignments to complete during our brief stay on earth. At the same time, while we temporarily reside in this world, we're to guard against becoming entangled in it. Instead, we're to live as "strangers and exiles on the earth" (Heb. 11:13) as we "set [our] mind[s] on the things above" (Col. 3:2).

Preparing for our journey to heaven means that because we understand what awaits us, we take the necessary steps while we await our destination. I hope over the course of this study, these steps have come into clearer focus for you.

This week we'll get a glimpse of the glory and blessings that await us when we've reached our final destination. Anticipating that day with joy and hope should shape the way we live the rest of our lives.

DAY 1
THE JUDGMENT

Let's begin our final week of study by understanding the two passages that speak of the two judgments to come. The first, the great white throne judgment, refers to God's judgment of unbelievers:

> *I saw a great white throne and Him who sat upon it, from whose presence earth and heaven fled away, and no place was found for them. And I saw the dead, the great and the small, standing before the throne, and books were opened; and another book was opened, which is the book of life; and the dead were judged from the things which were written in the books, according to their deeds. And the sea gave up the dead which were in it, and death and Hades gave up the dead which were in them; and they were judged, every one of them according to their deeds. Then death and Hades were thrown into the lake of fire. This is the second death, the lake of fire. And if anyone's name was not found written in the book of life, he was thrown into the lake of fire.*

REVELATION 20:11-15

At the great white throne judgment described here, people who haven't trusted in Christ will be expelled from His presence forever. Believers, however, have a greater future:

> *We must all appear before the judgment seat of Christ,*
> *so that each one may be recompensed for his deeds in the*
> *body, according to what he has done, whether good or bad.*

2 CORINTHIANS 5:10

This judgment, called the judgment seat of Christ, is strictly reserved for believers. Jesus will evaluate our works not for our eternal destiny but for the purpose of our rewards in heaven.

At the great white throne judgment, those who've rejected Jesus Christ will receive condemnation. At the judgment seat of Christ, followers of Jesus will receive commendation, for "there is now no condemnation for those who are in Christ Jesus" (Rom. 8:1).

A Place Called Heaven

Remember this simple but vitally important statement:

> The judgment seat of Christ is for the commendation of believers, while the great white throne judgment is for the condemnation of unbelievers.

How does understanding the reality of judgment for both believers and unbelievers affect you as a Christian?

Although you may have thought about judgment only as it relates to people who haven't trusted Jesus, judgment applies to both believers and unbelievers. The reality of judgment should both sober us because nonbelievers will be condemned and cause us to be grateful because believers will be commended.

Let's take a closer look at what awaits believers at the judgment seat of Christ. Most likely this evaluation will occur right after the rapture of the church, when living Christians will immediately be transported into the presence of the Lord and all believers who've previously died will be resurrected to eternal life. Although no single verse indicates that this judgment will occur immediately after the rapture, a couple of factors point to this conclusion.

1. The twenty-four elders mentioned in Revelation 4:10, who represent all believers, are portrayed as having already received their rewards (crowns) in heaven at the beginning of the tribulation.
2. When the church, the bride of Christ, returns to the earth with Jesus at the second coming seven years after the rapture, the bride is said to be clothed in "fine linen, bright and clean," which represents "the righteous acts of the saints" (Rev. 19:8).

Both of these facts imply that the evaluation of Christians' lives has already occurred.

How have explanations of events in the Book of Revelation made these often difficult passages more personal for you?

What will actually happen at the judgment seat of Christ? Paul used three analogies to teach this truth.

1. A TRUST AGREEMENT WITH GOD

You, why do you judge your brother? Or you again, why do
you regard your brother with contempt? For we will all stand
before the judgment seat of God. For it is written,
"As I live, says the Lord, every knee shall bow to Me,
And every tongue shall give praise to God."
So then each one of us will give an account of himself to God.

ROMANS 14:10-12

The idea of giving an account is built on the analogy of a trustee—someone who's responsible and legally bound to administer something that belongs to another person. At some future time the trustee must give an account of the way he or she managed that trust. For example, financial advisers serve as trustees of their clients' money. The money these advisers invest doesn't belong to them; they're simply managers who oversee and hopefully multiply the owners' funds.

Similarly, everything we possess, internally and externally, is a trust from God. We're only stewards or managers of the assets God has granted us. Therefore, it's only right and fair that one day He will ask, "What have you done with the resources I've entrusted you with?" We'll be judged only by the opportunities we were given, not in comparison to anyone else. It's not a competition but an evaluation.

What are your assets and gifts?	How are you using them to multiply the kingdom?

How does the analogy of a trustee change the way you view what God has given you?

2. CONSTRUCTING A HOUSE OF GOD

According to the grace of God which was given to me, like a wise master builder I laid a foundation, and another is building on it. But each man must be careful how he builds on it. For no man can lay a foundation other than the one which is laid, which is Jesus Christ. Now if any man builds on the foundation with gold, silver, precious stones, wood, hay, straw, each man's work will become evident; for the day will show it because it is to be revealed with fire, and the fire itself will test the quality of each man's work. If any man's work which he has built on it remains, he will receive a reward. If any man's work is burned up, he will suffer loss; but he himself will be saved, yet so as through fire.

1 CORINTHIANS 3:10-15

The idea Paul conveyed is that our lives are a house, and our faith has built a solid foundation on Christ. As we lived, did we build with eternal or temporary materials? Every aspect of our lives that's judged to be temporal rather than eternal will be consumed in the inferno of God's holiness, leaving behind only a pile of ashes. But building a life that glorifies God and loves our neighbors constructs a house that will endure and will be rewarded.

Prayerfully record activities in your life that you know are building a durable, eternal spiritual house.

3. RUNNING A RACE FOR CHRIST

Do you not know that those who run in a race all run, but only one receives the prize? Run in such a way that you may win. Everyone who competes in the games exercises self-control in all things. They then do it to receive a perishable wreath, but we an imperishable. Therefore I run in such a way, as not without aim; I box in such a way, as not beating the air; but I discipline my body and make it my slave, so that, after I have preached to others, I myself will not be disqualified.

1 CORINTHIANS 9:24-27

Through the analogy of a race, Paul teaches us several truths about a Christian life worthy of receiving imperishable rewards.

- The race begins when the official fires the starting gun. We begin our race of faith the moment we placed our eternal trust in Christ.
- Runners must stay on the track or be disqualified. Christians have a unique course God has designed for us that has no shortcuts.
- Runners must avoid distractions and keep their eyes on the finish line. Christians must avoid worldly distractions and must discipline themselves to keep their eyes on Jesus.

What's one area of your life with which you continually struggle that keeps you from running the best race you can?

To be ready for the great white throne judgment, be certain you have a relationship with Christ. To be ready for the judgment seat of Christ, become a wise trustee, carefully choose your building materials each day, and constantly let go of the baggage that can slow you down in running your race.

PRAYER

Lord Jesus, make me a wiser steward of all You've entrusted to me. Lead me to choose eternal materials as I build my house in You. Help me throw off anything that hinders me from running my race for the imperishable prize You've promised me. I long to hear You say one day, "Well done, good and faithful servant!" In Your name, amen.

DAY 2
WINNERS & LOSERS

Many Christians think they'll be relieved that they get to go to heaven, but we must remember that conversion is just the beginning of a new life in Christ. On the great day when we arrive in heaven, we'll be grateful for every moment we spent focusing on God's will and on what He called us to do (see Rev. 20:12).

In God's kingdom, rewards make sense because God is just. Believers who've spent their lives fully devoted to Him will have great fruit from their labor, with many people led to Jesus and many Christians matured in the faith. That fruit will be recognized and rewarded, in contrast to those who spent very little time investing in and ministering to others. Keep in mind that we're talking about believers' works for heavenly rewards, not works for salvation.

> What causes us to be complacent and apathetic about living for God's purposes instead of remembering that Jesus is coming back to take us to heaven and reward us for the fruit of our lives?

> Why do so many people, including Christians, confuse choosing to work for rewards with having to work for salvation?

WHAT THE WINNERS WIN

What if you trained for years to run in a marathon and on race day you took first place? Then what if the race organizers told you that rather than giving trophies to the top ten runners, they were going to give everyone a participation trophy? Would you feel that decision was fair? Would you question why you had spent all that time and energy training? That's exactly why God gives rewards to believers according to how well they ran the race. Let's explore the meanings of the five crowns that the Bible specifies as rewards for Christians who ran the race well.

CROWN 1: IMPERISHABLE

Everyone who competes in the games exercises self-control in all things.
They then do it to receive a perishable wreath, but we an imperishable.

1 CORINTHIANS 9:25

This heavenly crown is for believers who have lived lives that are—

- disciplined;
- fruitful;
- productive;
- Spirit-controlled.

Consider your spiritual life and identify one area in which you know you exercise these qualities. Then record an area in which you need to grow.

How will you improve?

CROWN 2: EXULTATION

Who is our hope or joy or crown of exultation? Is it not even you, in the
presence of our Lord Jesus at His coming? For you are our glory and joy.

1 THESSALONIANS 2:19-20

This heavenly crown is for believers who invest in—

- intentional relationships;
- evangelism;
- discipleship.

These winners have dedicated time and energy to populating heaven and growing God's children to maturity.

Most Christians tend to lean toward either evangelism or discipleship. Identify your stronger ministry and why you answered with that choice.

CROWN 3: RIGHTEOUSNESS

In the future there is laid up for me the crown of righteousness, which the Lord, the righteous Judge, will award to me on that day; and not only to me, but also to all who have loved His appearing.

2 TIMOTHY 4:8

This heavenly crown is for believers who live in—
- anticipation of Christ's return;
- obedience;
- faithfulness.

What's one practical step you can take to focus more on your crown of righteousness?

CROWN 4: LIFE

Blessed is a man who perseveres under trial; for once he has been approved, he will receive the crown of life which the Lord has promised to those who love Him.

JAMES 1:12

This heavenly crown is for believers who stay focused on—
- enduring trials;
- overcoming persecution;
- withstanding the enemy's attacks.

Record any trial or hardship you're enduring solely because of your faith in Christ. What are you learning from this trial?

CROWN 5: GLORY

When the Chief Shepherd appears, you
will receive the unfading crown of glory.

1 PETER 5:4

This heavenly crown is for believers who invest in—

- serving the church;
- shepherding people;
- teaching God's Word.

This crown isn't just for professional ministers. Identify any way you faithfully serve the church, shepherd people, or teach the Word.

WHAT THE LOSERS LOSE

Scripture warns believers about the possibility of losing rewards:

Watch yourselves, that you do not lose what we have
accomplished, but that you may receive a full reward.

2 JOHN 8

If any man's work is burned up, he will suffer loss;
but he himself will be saved, yet so as through fire.

1 CORINTHIANS 3:15

What changes do you need to make in your life to take more seriously the prospect of gaining eternal rewards?

Not everyone will experience the same degree of joy and satisfaction in heaven. Though our salvation is secure, the loss of heavenly rewards would result in genuine regret. Often we think of heaven as being a place of uniform happiness, but rejoicing and regret aren't mutually exclusive.

Many Christians will experience that mixture of joy and regret at the judgment seat of Christ. Though they'll be eternally grateful for their escape from the lake of fire, they'll also experience regret as they watch their lives go up in smoke when God judges their works as worthless. When they arrive at the judgment seat of Christ, it will become abundantly clear that much of what they thought they did for Christ, they actually did for themselves. These works won't merit eternal rewards. As a result, they'll experience a sense of loss as they realize the rewards they've forfeited. However, once the Lord has finished His evaluation, whatever tears may have been shed will be gone forever, even though the forfeiture of rewards will have eternal consequences.

To be unconcerned with heavenly rewards is to make faithfulness to God in this life irrelevant. On the other hand, to make too much of earning heavenly rewards is to embrace legalism. Our goal as believers is to faithfully and diligently run the race God has set before us, to handle our trust with care, and to build our lives with actions and motives that have eternal value.

PRAYER

Heavenly Father, the fact that You'll not only save sinners who repent but also reward us for our commitment to your kingdom here on earth is miraculous. Thank You for being a good and gracious Father. In Christ's name, amen.

DAY 3

DON'T FEAR DEATH

Winston Churchill, who faced death on many occasions during his legendary life, once quipped, "Any man who says he is not afraid of death is a liar."[1] One reason Christians may fear death is that they're unaware of exactly what awaits them on the other side of it. But there are three reasons Christians don't need to fear death.

1. IF YOU'RE A CHRISTIAN, YOU CAN BE ASSURED THAT YOU WON'T DEPART THIS EARTH ONE SECOND BEFORE GOD'S APPOINTED TIME. Paul said David didn't die until he had accomplished God's purpose in the generation appointed for him to live (see Acts 13:36). When his work on earth was completed, God took Him home. The same is true for you.

David looked to God as his solace in the face of any fear:

> *The LORD is my light and my salvation;*
> *Whom shall I fear?*
> *The LORD is the defense of my life;*
> *Whom shall I dread?*
>
> PSALM 27:1

Are you afraid of death? If so, identify the primary reason. What reasons does Psalm 27:1 give to trust God more than you fear death?

If you fear death on any level, how could focusing on the truths of God's Word about the realities of heaven help you minimize that fear?

2. FROM GOD'S PERSPECTIVE, NO ONE DIES PREMATURELY; GOD ALONE DETERMINES THE NUMBER OF OUR DAYS. When a young person dies tragically or a celebrity dies suddenly, we sometimes hear comments like "He died way before his time," "Gone much too soon," or "She still had so many great years in front of her."

This mindset reflects a worldview espousing that life as well as death is often an accident, so we're surprised and caught off guard when everyone doesn't live to old age. Although tragic and sudden deaths create legitimate questions and grief, we must hold on to the truth that God is in control and has a purpose. David determined to trust God in the face of that reality:

> *As for me, I trust in You, O LORD,*
> *I say, "You are my God."*
> *My times are in Your hand;*
> *Deliver me from the hand of my enemies*
> *and from those who persecute me.*
> *Make Your face to shine upon Your servant;*
> *Save me in Your lovingkindness.*
>
> PSALM 31:14-16

Why should we trust God with our days and make the most of them?

Although the news of someone's death can shock and surprise us, God is never surprised. People who die in faith—whether at nine or ninety—live exactly the number of years God prescribed for them. As someone once said, "Every person is immortal until his or her work on earth is done." Paul wrote about God's purpose for those who are in Christ:

> *Also we have obtained an inheritance, having been predestined*
> *according to His purpose who works all things after the*
> *counsel of His will, to the end that we who were the first*
> *to hope in Christ would be to the praise of His glory.*
>
> EPHESIANS 1:11-12

God has a purpose for every part of our lives. He knows the number of our days and has given us the Holy Spirit as an inheritance to live faithfully with the time He has given us. No believer dies prematurely. All Christians live until God's purpose is fulfilled.

Why do you suppose most people react to any death that's sudden or tragic as a mistake or an accident?

How can you better incorporate the sense of accomplishing God's purpose into your daily life?

3. DEATH IS A NECESSARY TRANSITION FROM THIS WORLD TO THE NEXT. Here's a comforting thought to consider about death: the only way to get to heaven is to die. For Christians, death is merely a transition to a new life—a simple realm change. Death is a transition from an inferior station to a superior destination. Paul wrote:

> *Flesh and blood cannot inherit the kingdom of God;*
> *nor does the perishable inherit the imperishable.*
>
> 1 CORINTHIANS 15:50

Our earthly bodies are designed for life here but aren't suitable for life in heaven. Death provides this necessary change to bodies that are suited for heaven. Death separates us from our earthly bodies so that we can put on our new bodies. God has invited every Christian to a magnificent location for which we must be properly dressed, and He has provided the appropriate wardrobe. Death is nothing more than exchanging inferior clothing for superior clothing.

The inheritance Paul referred to happens fully when we die. For believers, death means inheriting a new, richer beginning.

How can you adopt a new way of thinking to replace your past paradigm of death with transitional concepts of a new destination, new clothing, and inheriting an imperishable reward?

The reality is that even strong, committed Christians will still fear the unknown of death and will regret what they'll miss on the earth, while others will face death with courage and anticipation of their new home. Regardless, we can be assured that what awaits all believers will be far better and far more glorious than anything this earth could ever offer.

If we fear the day of death as it draws near, we can be comforted by recalling Jesus' words to the thief who was also enduring the pain of crucifixion: "Truly I say to you, today you shall be with Me in Paradise" (Luke 23:43). We too are dying, but soon we'll be with our Savior in our heavenly home.

Close today's study by reading other comforting words of Christ about what we have to look forward to:

> *Blessed are you who hunger now, for you shall be satisfied.*
> *Blessed are you who weep now, for you shall laugh.*

LUKE 6:21

PRAYER

Lord Jesus, thank You for giving me so many courageous and comforting words in Scripture about my transition to my new home, new clothes, and inheritance with You forever. Give me a healthy perspective on death and help me focus on living the way You intend for me until the day You choose to take me home. In Your name, amen.

---

1. Winston Churchill, as quoted in James C. Humes, *The Wit and Wisdom of Winston Churchill* (New York: HarperCollins, 1994), 25.

DAY 4

MAKE THE MOST OF
YOUR TIME, PART 1

The idea of a bucket list began to sweep through our culture in the early to mid-2000s, finally becoming a household term after the popular movie of the same name was released in 2007. The term originated from the decision about what we want to do in life before we kick the bucket, that is, die. The meaning of this phrase is thought to derive from an attempt to commit suicide by hanging. With a rope around the neck, a person stands on a bucket and then kicks it away in order to die.

Since the introduction of the bucket list to our entertainment-crazed society, tens of thousands of people have written bucket lists and then have begun the journey of fulfilling the items and checking them off. From seeing the Grand Canyon to skydiving to finally buying that motorcycle or recreational vehicle, people want to accomplish their dreams and goals before they die.

Is there anything inherently wrong with this concept? No, but the very sad and unfortunate fact about so many of those who start the journey of fulfilling a bucket list is that they have no idea where they'll spend eternity and often no thought as to what lies ahead following death.

Why do you suppose the idea of the bucket list has spread throughout Western culture over the past few years?

Read Jesus' words about what constitutes fulfilling life:

> *I am the door; if anyone enters through Me, he will be saved, and will go in and out and find pasture. The thief comes only to steal and kill and destroy; I came that they may have life, and have it abundantly.*

> JOHN 10:9-10

Record a few ways your life became abundant or full after you entered a relationship with Jesus.

A Place Called Heaven

In light of Jesus' words, what might He want to write on your bucket list?

The younger we are, the more slowly time seems to go by. Waiting to get our driver's license seems like decades. Waiting to graduate from high school feels like far more than four years. The same is true of a college education. Once engaged, the wedding day can feel like an eternity away. But as the years go by, oddly, their speed seems to increase. When we know Jesus, all of our days can be filled with abundance and meaning. Knowing Jesus is a call to walk in a way that honors Him:

Be careful how you walk, not as unwise men but as wise,
making the most of your time, because the days are evil.

EPHESIANS 5:15-16

Paul's words convey a mixture of warning and encouragement. In the Bible the concept of walking is a metaphor for living. And whatever consumes your time determines how you walk—the way you live. We live in an age of distraction; we must fight for the priorities that have eternal importance.

List your top three priorities in life.

1.

2.

3.

Over the next few days, track how much of your time you spend on these three priorities. The end goal is to help you answer the practical question, *Am I walking or spending my time on the pursuits I deem to be most important in my life?*

We all make different and widely varying amounts of money, but we each get 168 hours a week—24 hours a day times 7 days a week. While money is a strong divider, time is the great equalizer.

In Ephesians 5:15-16 Paul contrasted wise and unwise ways of living. As a smart buyer or a sharp merchant must make the best of every opportunity in the market-place, Paul encourages believers to make the best possible use of our resources. Literally, the phrase "making the most of your time" (v. 16) means to buy up the time you need. The days are wicked, so don't be unwise and waste your opportunities.

What wasted opportunities do you imagine people might regret on their deathbeds?

What's one step you can take to make wise decisions with the limited time you have so that you don't end life with regrets?

As you've completed this study, in what ways has God called you to take action? If so, what steps will you take?

Make no mistake: Satan will do whatever it takes to prevent you from living a purposeful, God-honoring life. Satan will entice you to squander your time—and therefore your life—on worthless pursuits rather than invest it in God-given priorities. We'll consider these priorities in day 5.

PRAYER

Father God, thank You for the days You've given me. Help me make the most of them with the limited time I have. All of my time is Your time, and all of my life is open to Your will and guidance. In Christ's name, amen.

DAY 5

MAKE THE MOST OF YOUR TIME, PART 2

To make the most of our time, we first have to know where our time goes. The ways we spend our time and our money reveal where we're focusing our hearts.

Below is a list of activities that are pervasive time wasters in our culture. Estimate how much time you spend on these activities each week. Then prayerfully ask God whether you need to make adjustments or give up certain activities in order to make the most of your time on earth.

Activity	Time Spent Each Week	Adjustments You Need to Make
Facebook		
Other social media		
Reading/watching news		
Internet browsing		
Gaming (phone or video)		
Texting		
Television (including streaming)		

Notice that all of these activities are part of the digital world. All of them have become real threats to human interaction and relationships. I doubt that while lying on his or her deathbed, anyone will wish they had spend more time online, regardless of the activity. Instead, they'll regret their failure to establish; build; and grow connections with family, friends, and unbelievers.

This isn't a blanket condemnation of our digital world but rather a warning that God wants us to pursue interests and activities that strengthen our relationships with Him and other people. Those relationships are the source of almost all of God's plan for us on earth as we get ready for heaven.

As a result of this study, how will you seek to maximize the rest of your time on earth?

To maximize the time you have left, what adjustments do you need to make in your schedule and priorities?

As we've thought about our journey to heaven, I hope you've been challenged and encouraged. All the Bible teaches about heaven is meant to cause us to think differently about our lives on earth. Learning about heaven is a worthy endeavor, but allowing our thoughts of heaven to shape the way we live is the goal of our study together. In the coming weeks and months, look for ways you can put into practice all you've learned about a place called heaven.

Whom have you told about the hope of heaven since you've been a part of this study? With whom do you need to follow up?

Summarize the most important truth you learned during this study.

PRAYER

Take a moment to voice your own prayer to the Lord, expressing whatever comes to mind. Then take a moment to be still and know that He is God, inviting and allowing Him to speak to your heart.

SUPPLEMENTAL ARTICLES

A NEW HEAVEN AND A NEW EARTH

Throughout the Scriptures God is proclaimed and praised as the One who creates (see Gen. 1:1) and gives purpose to all creation (see Rev. 4:11). The creative character and purposes of God find ultimate biblical expression in John's vision recorded in Revelation 21, when he saw "a new heaven and a new earth" (v. 1). How would John's readers have understood his words? What would they have thought about a new heaven and a new earth? What significance does John's vision of a new heaven and a new earth have for us today?

The phrase "a new heaven and a new earth" wasn't original with John. The phrase first appears in Isaiah 65:17, when the prophet received a divine word of encouragement to share with Israel following its release from Babylonian captivity. Isaiah proclaimed a future hope rooted in what God was doing:

> *The former troubles are forgotten,*
> *And ... are hidden from My sight!*
> *For behold, I create new heavens and a new earth;*
> *And the former things will not be remembered or come to mind.*
> *But be glad and rejoice forever in what I create;*
> *For behold, I create Jerusalem for rejoicing*
> *And her people for gladness.*

ISAIAH 65:16-18

A similar use of the phrase is found in Isaiah 66, where, following God's judgment on His enemies, those who worship the Lord will gather from "all nations and tongues" (v. 18) at the "holy mountain Jerusalem" as "an offering to the LORD" (v. 20, NLT). God then promised:

> *"Just as the new heavens and the new earth*
> *Which I make will endure before Me," declares the LORD,*
> *"So your offspring and your name will endure."*

ISAIAH 66:22

The people of God, gathered from all nations, will themselves be an offering presented to God in Jerusalem. Both passages link a proclamation of God's glory and majesty to a creative work of God ("new earth"), with Jerusalem serving as the centerpiece of a restored relationship between God and humanity.

The wording of Isaiah 65:17-18 supports this link as God's creative work ("new heavens and a new earth," v. 17) finds tangible expression in God's intention to:

> *… create Jerusalem for rejoicing*
> *And her people for gladness.*[1]

ISAIAH 65:18

In short, the phrase "a new heaven and a new earth" portrays a time when God's people, delivered from bondage, will enjoy a renewed, intimate relationship with God as was intended in the exodus from Egypt.[2] For John's readers, no doubt familiar with the exodus and Isaiah's writings, references to the new heaven and the new earth would bring to mind a redemption scene rich in the fulfillment of such themes as the covenant and the return from exile.[3]

1. Pilchan Lee, *The New Jerusalem in the Book of Revelation* (Tübingen, Germany: Mohr Siebeck, 2001), 19.
2. David Mathewson, *A New Heaven and a New Earth* (London: Sheffield Academic, 2003), 68.
3. Ibid., 69.

Article adapted from Lynn O. Traylor, "A New Heaven and a New Earth," *Biblical Illustrator,* summer 2008, 54–56.

PARADISE

The English word *paradise* can be traced to an ancient Persian word that achieved international circulation.[1] The word originally referred to any enclosure. Later it came to refer to a park surrounded by a wall.[2] It was transliterated into Greek, Hebrew, and Aramaic. The earliest Greek use of the word referred to the park of a Persian king. The word could also refer to any park in general.

In Genesis 2–3 the phrase "garden of Eden" is consistently translated in the Septuagint, the Greek translation of the Old Testament, by the Greek word *paradeisos*. This religious use of *paradeisos* to refer to the garden of Eden affected later Jewish understanding of the word.

In Luke 23 as Jesus was dying on the cross, His enemies taunted Him for being able to save others but not Himself. One thief selfishly cursed Jesus. The other thief, perhaps impressed by Jesus' prayer of forgiveness, recognized that Jesus was the Messiah and that one day Jesus could come in power. "Jesus," he said, "remember me when You come in Your kingdom!" (v. 42). To his surprise, Jesus offered more than the thief could have hoped for by promising that the dying thief would join Him in paradise that day (see v. 43). Jesus' promise makes several matters clear.

1. Rewards and punishments begin immediately after death, and those rewards include fellowship with Jesus. This teaching is in line with other statements in the New Testament. Lazarus immediately went to paradise, the rich man immediately to Hades (see Luke 16:22-23). Paul taught that to be absent from the body was to be present with the Lord (see 2 Cor. 5:8).
2. The state the penitent thief entered was a conscious state, not soul sleep. If Jesus had been referring to a state of unconsciousness that would last until the second coming, His promise "Today you shall be with Me in Paradise" (Luke 23:43) would have had no meaning. Jesus promised the penitent thief that he would experience the blessed state that day.
3. *Paradise* is a way of referring to heaven. Being in paradise is being with Jesus in perfect fellowship with God. Paradise is heaven, not a rest stop along the way.

The penitent thief acknowledged his sin and asked for forgiveness in the last hours of his life. He had nothing to commend himself except his faith in Jesus. That was enough. He had begun that day walking with Jesus to the hill called the Skull. By faith he would end that day walking with Jesus into God's presence.

1. Harvey K. McArthur, "Paradise," *The Interpreter's Dictionary of the Bible*, vol. 3 (Nashville: Abingdon, 1962), 655.
2. Joachim Jeremias, "Paradeisos," *Theological Dictionary of the New Testament*, vol. 5 (Grand Rapids, MI: Eerdmans, 1967), 765.

Article adapted from Charles A. Ray, "Paradise," *Biblical Illustrator*, winter 1994, 65–67.

JUDGMENT AND REWARDS

The New Testament clearly declares that God has set a day to adjudicate the deeds and decisions of every person (see Acts 17:31; Rom. 2:16; 1 Cor. 4:5; 1 John 4:17). Jesus stated, "The Father … has given all judgment to the Son. … He who does not honor the Son does not honor the Father who sent Him" (John 5:22-23). Unlike a human court, which occasionally makes a serious mistake and fails to exercise proper justice, judgment by the "Sovereign Lord" (Rev. 6:10, NLT) will be pure, full of truth, inerrant, thorough, and complete.

In what manner, however, will believers be judged? Will they face the same scrutiny that unbelievers face? Indeed, the New Testament testifies that "each one of us will give an account of himself to God" (Rom. 14:12) and that "we must all appear before the judgment seat of Christ, so that each one may be recompensed for his deeds in the body, according to what he has done, whether good or bad" (2 Cor. 5:10). Similarly, Matthew 16:24-28 and 1 Peter 4:1-2,12-19 underscore the judgment that will come to believers as "the household of God" (1 Pet. 4:17). Jesus will examine all, "according to his deeds" (Matt. 16:27). Do these verses indicate that works are essential to salvation and that human performance can earn God's favor? In a word, no.

When eager seekers asked Jesus what they could do to perform the works of God, Jesus replied, "This is the work of God, that you believe in Him whom He has sent" (John 6:29). Although all individuals will be subject to God's comprehensive examination, the fundamental act of justification by grace through faith makes the eternal, definitive difference for people who believe in Jesus. Believers are justified by faith as the New Testament asserts, but they're judged by their fruit. Although works don't earn salvation, they give evidence of salvation. A believer's works that are most pleasing to God are those done in faith with a conviction that there's no merit other than what Christ alone accomplishes through us. Consequently, the New Testament doesn't even imply that salvation depends on a person's service for God.[1]

Although judgment carries a serious punitive aspect, is also carries a positive recompense for faithful believers. The role of rewards highlights the benefits of obedience to Christ and encourages believers to be persistent through life's hardships and fiery trials. God bestows rewards in His future kingdom for both a disposition of Christlikeness and a demonstration of devotion to Christ's glory. Rewards to believers are intended to reflect the worthiness of Jesus working in and through the individual.[2]

1. Donald Guthrie, *New Testament Theology* (Downers Grove, IL: InterVarsity, 1981), 362.
2. Ruth M. Fuller, "Rewards," *Dictionary of Paul and His Letters*, ed. Gerald F. Hawthorne, Ralph P. Martin, and Daniel G. Reid (Downers Grove, IL: InterVarsity, 1993), 819–20.

Article adapted from M. Dean Register, "Judgment and Reward," *Biblical Illustrator*, spring 2015, 71–74.

Because . . .

. . . you really do want to go deeper

What were marriage customs like in Jesus' day? Exactly who were the Hittites, and what did they have to do with David? What was so alluring about those carved idols?

If these are the types of topics that intrigue you, *Biblical Illustrator* is for you! This quarterly magazine explores the customs, history, peoples, and archaeology of the biblical world—and more. Each issue offers over 20 articles that can help you go deeper in your Bible study. *Biblical Illustrator*—it's the treasure you've been looking for. Order yours today!

To order, call 800-458-2772 or go online to lifeway.com/biblicalillustrator